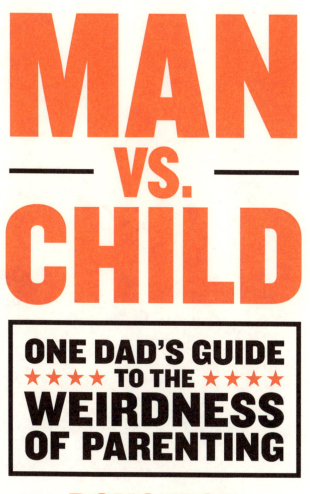

MAN
— VS. —
CHILD

ONE DAD'S GUIDE
★★★★ **TO THE** ★★★★
WEIRDNESS
OF PARENTING

DOUG MOE

ILLUSTRATIONS BY JORDAN AWAN

Abrams, New York

CONTENTS

INTRODUCTION

You are looking for a book about being a dad. A book that helps you with sleep training, feedings, and teaching your child the values that your parents instilled in you.

That book was sold out, though. So now you are holding this one: *Man vs. Child*.

Well it's your lucky day, because that other book was *boring*. That other book seemed so helpful, but it was going to take twenty pages to tell you how to not get poo on yourself. That other book seemed so informative, but it was going to go on and on about brain development but not how to deal with a screaming toddler having a meltdown in the American Museum of Natural History.

That other book was going to make you want to gouge your eyes out and cry, *"Why?! Why torture me with this terrible book when all I wanted was to be a good parent?!"* I hate that book and what it has done to you. You're a wreck. Get a hold of yourself!

This book is different. *Man vs. Child* is about the absurdity of being a dad today: from your blissful pre-baby days through when your kid is off at school, probably talking shit about you. It's a companion to help you through the hard times, like when you need something to read on the toilet and your phone is dead.

It's a guidebook for smart, funny dads like you who are still worried about messing up their kids.

Because that's where we are these days, right? We're supposed to be New Dads—more involved and emotionally available—but no one told us how. Old Dads could pull a Don Draper: send money to the wife and kids and generally half-ass it from afar. But New Dads play dress-up, bake, and diaper, all while trying to keep it together. If you're a new dad, you need a book that will give you a little practical advice, but mostly lets you know that your kid isn't winning and that *you've still got it, champ.*

I won't condescend to you or make this book look like some kind of computer user manual to trick you into learning about being a dad. On the other hand, I may not provide a ton of medical advice. Oh, you wanted medical advice? All right, go ahead and buy that other book, just in case. No, it's fine. I get it. I'll wait here.

For now, know this: You have done the right thing by buying this book. Or you have done the wrong thing by stealing this book. If you borrowed this book, that seems fair. If you borrowed it from the library, but have never returned it, *shame on you.*

WHO AM I?

I'm Doug Moe. I'm a comedian based at the legendary Upright Citizens Brigade Theatre, where I am a long-time teacher and performer. I live in Brooklyn, the epicenter of artisanal mayonnaise and the Mustache Renaissance.

In 2006, I became a dad. (You know how that happens, right? Because I don't want to explain it.) And because being an actor/comedian/writer is a verified sketchy way to make a living, I was also a part-time stay-at-home dad. Ya know, a PTSAHD. I also started writing funny stuff for the Internet, including my own blog, predictably named *Man Versus Child*, which led to this book.

And because I was basically a perfect dad, my daughter is perfect and everything is perfect.

Now you can enjoy the fruits of my perfection.

Okay, maybe I'm exaggerating. Maybe I actually didn't know what the hell I was doing. Maybe I was lucky enough to fumble through it with a lot of help from my wonderful wife. And maybe I managed to do a lot of things wrong but have done enough things right that my daughter is ten years old now and only yells at me for ruining her life every OTHER day.

And I'm sure that there's a lot that I still don't know. Living in Brooklyn, I'm missing out on whole sections of the child-rearing experience, such as dealing with drive-throughs, for example. And I have a daughter, so I haven't dealt with a lot of "smashing the two toys together until they break" like my friends with sons have. Of course, when I was a kid, I destroyed a bunch of my Hot Wheels cars with a hammer, so I know a couple things. And I'm lucky enough to have a great wife who did more than half of the parenting and kept our family sane. So I've never been a single parent, which must be insane.

But a lot of parenting is the same, whether you are in Akron, Ohio, or on Avenue A. If it's helpful, substitute *artisanal mayonnaise* for *BBQ sauce* where necessary. I'm just one dad, but I can help you. A little.

What I'm saying is: I've been there, pal. Now, let's talk about your fun, worthless life without a child.

WHO SHOULD BUY THIS BOOK?

★ Guys about to have babies

★ Ladies about to have babies

★ Wise-guy friends of a guy who thought he got someone pregnant

★ Brothers-in-law especially worried about fathers-to-be

★ Mothers-to-be especially worried that their fathers-in-law forgot to get a gift for their husbands/fathers-to-be

★ Mothers-in-law, fathers-to-be, sisters-in-law, brothers-to-be . . . basically the whole in-law/to-be category

★ People looking for a bargain, assuming this has ended up on a bargain table somewhere

★ People looking for a book, any book, to look book smart

★ Billionaires with money to burn

★ Book burners without books to burn

★ Someone looking to learn the English language who also wants to laugh—and maybe cry a little—and definitely learn something

★ You, a person who likes lists, in case none of the above applies

CHAPTER ONE

MAN ★ VS. ★ LIFE

YOUR FUN, WORTHLESS LIFE WITHOUT A CHILD

"WHY AM I HERE?"

That's the big question that hits you when you're boozing your way through a wonderful brunch with close friends.

"What's it all for?"
That's the other question. The one that hits you as you scarf down a bite of delicious eggs Florentine. This big question has been pondered ever since man stopped doodling on cave walls and started thinking about work/life balance.

"What is my purpose?"
Oof. Now, *that's a question.* Is your purpose brunch? Or your band? Your job? Do you even *have* a job?! You have incredible freedom, but for what? What do you do with it? You while away your time watching TV or collecting comic books. You sleep in. You waste it all.

- ★ What if I took away your late-night hot wings but gave your life meaning?
- ★ What if I took away your freedom but gave you a higher purpose?
- ★ What if I took away peace and quiet but gave you laughter, then crying, then whining, but then laughter again?

That's what being a dad is like: It gives you meaning and purpose and fills your days with laughter, then crying, then whining, but then laughter again. You're welcome.

MAYBE YOU WILL BE A GREAT DAD NOW THAT WE KNOW YOU'RE NOT A GREAT GUITARIST

By now, you're old enough to have failed at many things. You know you're never going to be a great guitarist or a professional gamer. Your videos never went viral. But you could be a great dad. Isn't that more noble than being good at guitar? Isn't that more meaningful than video games? You used to be insanely obsessed with Facebook likes, but you could be pouring that insanity into a *child*.

THERE ARE SEVERAL GOOD REASONS TO HAVE A KID

The main reason is that a kid is someone who, at least for a while, will really like you. Will love you. Will give you hugs and write sweet things to you and give you kisses. *I promised myself I wouldn't cry.*

And having a kid makes you a better person. I really think so. A friend of mine told me that before you have a kid, you think you have a set amount of love in your heart, but having a kid opens up a whole new chamber full of love you didn't know you had. It's like that weird dream where you discover you have another room in your apartment that you had forgotten about. It's not like that weird dream where your head is made of bologna but no one told you.

Ready to have a baby? No? Well, let's take this piece by piece. What are "babies"?

WHAT ARE "BABIES"?

C'mon, you know what a baby is, so cut the crap.

No?

Okay, so you're not a baby guy. I gotcha. That's okay. Lots of great dads are not baby guys to start. There's still hope.

You've seen babies all over the place, but never really thought too much about them, fine. I, too, was like this when I was *Un-Childed*. Un-Childed people are not yet enlightened, not yet blessed with the beauty of children. They are really not paying attention to babies. So what are "babies"? Let's make sure you know the answer.

Really, babies are just Tiny People. But here's a secret that no one tells you before you have one: Not all babies are the same.

Did I just blow your mind? Yes, some babies are older than others. And new babies and older babies are fundamentally different species. Roughly speaking, they break down like this:

- ★ **BABY, NEWBORN:** This is the kind of super-tiny baby that you see and think, *"WHOA, that is a tiny baby."*
- ★ **BABY, STANDARD-ISSUE:** This is a classic baby. Not too small, not too big. Not walking around, not talking. Just doing classic baby stuff, like drinking a bottle or throwing something on the floor.
- ★ **BABY, COOL:** This baby has a lot of personality. What a cool baby. I will also refer to this kind of baby as an "Interesting Baby."
- ★ **BABY, CRABBY:** This might be a toddler. Are they walking? Are they being kind of annoying? Probably a toddler.
- ★ **BABY, BIGGER, TALKED YOU INTO AN ELABORATE BANK HEIST WHEREIN YOU ARE PUSHING THIS BABY IN A STROLLER AND THEN IT POPPED OUT WITH A GUN AND DEMANDED MONEY:** This is probably a tiny gangster, not an actual baby. Check out my book *Man vs. Tiny Gangster.*

Now that you know what a baby is, the question is: Are you ready to have one?

ARE YOU READY TO HAVE A BABY?

No. But you're asking the wrong question. The right question is:

"ARE YOU *EVER* READY TO HAVE A BABY?"

If you're like me, you had a ton of things to do FIRST before having a baby. Things that would make you *ready*. Like:

★ being successful
★ being mature
★ having money
★ having a plan, for once
★ having enough room—I mean, we live in a one bedroom!
★ being not such a total screw-up, like *THAT'LL* ever happen
★ *feeling* ready

Being ready is overrated and can take forever.

SHOULDN'T I AT LEAST BE A GROWN-UP FIRST?

The answer again is no.

Here's a little pearl of actual wisdom that I've acquired from being a parent: You can be an adult without being a grown-up.

That is to say, you can be full-size without *feeling* like you are a grown-up. Grown-ups are serious. They are deeply settled into the world. They are self-assured and complete. When you're a kid, most adults seem this way, especially dads.

But as you become an adult, you realize that most of the adults you know aren't grown-ups. They don't know what the hell they're doing. Some bully from your high school becomes the town cop. Or your flaky college roommate who used to steal your hummus becomes a big TV producer. And yet they haven't changed a bit.

It turns out that everyone's a big fake, especially people who think they are grown-ups. No one is ever really a grown-up.

The good news is that you can be as big a liar as they all are! And if you become a parent, you'll have to be. So, no, you aren't a grown-up and you aren't "ready" to have a baby. Join the club.

SHOULD I HAVE A DOG FIRST?

This is a common thought: *I should have a dog before I have a baby. That way I can get used to caring for something else.* Good idea—you should have a dog first. But you can't just skip to the dog.

The proper sequence is:
1. Plant
2. Small bowl that you always put your keys in so you stop losing them
3. Fish
4. New plant (other plant died)
5. Cat (optional)
6. Another cat, so the first one has a friend
7. Shared Google Calendar that you and your wife actually check
8. New cat (don't ask)
9. Dog
10. Baby

ARE DOGS LIKE BABIES?

Dogs can be great practice for babies! And dogs and babies are more similar *now* than at any other time in history. Dogs have become more like babies. Both have:

- ★ Human names
- ★ Cute outfits
- ★ Strollers

And babies are more like dogs:

- ★ Dog names
- ★ Attempts to bring them into restaurants where they are not welcome
- ★ Good for about thirteen years, give or take

NO, DOGS ARE NOT LIKE BABIES

Despite these similarities, let me assure you that babies and dogs are not the same thing, no matter what your coworker Susan thinks.

Dogs won't:

- ★ Need money
- ★ Resent your jokes
- ★ Love you, then tolerate you, then resent you, then love you again

Babies won't:

- ★ Lick another baby's butt and then lick you
- ★ Bark and bark and bark at absolutely nothing, even when you say "NO!" a bunch of times
- ★ Dig in the dirt, roll around in a dead thing, and then whine about a bath. Well, probably not.

So sure, get a dog first. It can give you love and help you practice feeding something else regularly. And then a dog can be a useful companion to your baby, something else to terrorize and assert dominance over until you have a second child.

CHAPTER TWO

MAN ★ VS. ★ PREGNANCY

THE WEIRDNESS GROWS

PREGNANCY AND BIRTH: WHOA

Pregnancy is a weird, exciting time for you and your wife. When my wife got pregnant, it was the first time in awhile that we'd really had to plan something.

A few years before we had planned what I think everyone will agree was the best wedding ever. But that had been more of an exercise in budgeting and where to seat my dad's weird cousin than planning a new life. Deciding on cupcakes instead of a wedding cake felt pretty significant at the time, but in retrospect it pales in comparison to having a baby. Babies don't come in red velvet, for one thing.

Babies require even more planning. We had a lot to prepare for mentally and strategically. Would we stay in our one-bedroom, fourth-floor walk-up apartment? How could we save some money? What should we name this kid? Where should we put the crib?

All the planning was exciting, though. Imagining what it'd be like to be parents, to be "establishing a family"—it was all like our own little private joke or something. It felt like a fun secret, like when you're not wearing underwear.

And it snapped me to attention: I had to step up! Sure, every couple is supposed to take care of each other, and you *know* I'm the one rebooting the router when our Wi-Fi is down. But the physical realness of my wife's pregnant body made the whole thing a lot less theoretical. When your partner's not feeling well and her body is changing and she can feel a baby's elbow in her stomach—that tends to focus the mind.

Sounds crazy, right? You've got nine months or so to get your head in the game. Hop to it!

YOUR ROLE AS NON-PREGNANT GUY

Other books can tell you the medical stages of pregnancy. Those books are all "trimester this" and "trimester that." But for understanding what it'll be like for you, the bystander, refer to this handy summary.

STAGES OF PREGNANCY (AS OBSERVED FROM NEARBY)

1. Maybe pregnant, maybe not
2. Pregnant but superstitious
3. Pregnant but secret
4. Pregnant but passing for bloated
5. Definitely pregnant. Tell everyone! Classic pregnant.
6. Super-pregnant, probably can't get any bigger than that
7. WTF pregnant, watermelon-sideways pregnant, impossibly pregnant
8. Baby

SOME THINGS ARE NOT *FOR* YOU

Clearly there's a lot more to it. But some of this baby thing is going to be almost exclusively for your wife to experience: a person growing inside her body, a person coming out of her body, and breast-feeding to name just a few. Even the most sympathetically almost-pregnant dads-to-be have to satisfy themselves with descriptions of the bizarre inner workings of child growing.

BE A GREAT SIDEKICK

That doesn't make you useless. Some dads use their bystander status to justify not doing anything baby related. But I think you're a New

Dad. I think you should help in as many ways as you can and be a great sidekick. What's Batman without Robin? What's peanut butter without jelly?

Sidekicks are invaluable. Here's how you can help:

★ Put the crib together based on the rage-inducing instructions; pregnant women shouldn't hurl things.

★ Paint the baby's room so your baby doesn't get whacked out on paint fumes.

★ Go to the billion doctor's appointments and nod along, then look stuff up later.

★ Read up on pregnancy from other, more authoritative books so you don't look like you are just a cutup who only likes comedy books.

Sure, Robin's main job is to help fight the Joker and keep the Bat-mobile gassed up, but I bet Batman keeps him around for the awesome foot rubs, too. Sidekicks do what needs to be done.

BIRTH CLASS: WELCOME TO THE BODY

Maybe you lead a more interesting life than I do, but birth class was the first time I sat around with a bunch of dudes while we all rubbed our wives' bellies.

Birth class is where you reacquaint yourself with the physical. As you've gotten older, there've been hints that the body is weird (a long hair growing from the top of your ear; a zit that you squeeze and squeeze until you have to go to the doctor), but your wife's pregnancy is on a whole other level. And birth class is where you confront the weirdness of bodies head-on . . . through the vagina.

GREAT THINGS ABOUT PREGNANCY

Many people look back fondly on pregnancy. There are some great things about it:

★ Your wife has the "Glow" when she doesn't have the "Morning Sickness Green."

★ It's fun being with someone who is generally not in the mood to take any BS.

★ It's pretty cool to see something moving in another person's stomach that isn't an alien or something.

★ You finally get to be the big spoon in bed.

★ It's proof that your boys can swim, even though that's a stupid thing to be proud of.

★ You're finally allowed to talk to your wife's stomach without her getting mad.

★ You gain sympathy weight from many delicious sympathy sandwiches.

There are many different types of birth classes, but it's likely that you will be attending some kind of post-hippie birth-empowering class designed to give you lots of information so you feel more in control of a scary process.

These classes are totally worth doing so that you can bone up on epidurals, dilation, and contractions. You'll learn all of the technical stuff and all the options for birth, and you'll get to formulate a "birth plan."

A birth plan is your plan for how you and your wife would like the birth to go. It is like many plans you will have in the future: a great theory, largely scrapped as soon as the shit hits the fan.

MASSAGE YOUR WAY TO A NATURAL CHILDBIRTH

Nowadays, the goal is to have a "natural childbirth." Your wife will likely want to be "present" and hope to have the least amount of drugs necessary. To this end, you will learn a bunch of massages that are supposed to serve as an alternative to epidurals That said, most women don't yell for "less epidural" once they get a *taste*.

You'll also learn how to coach your wife's breathing: deep breaths, counting, and not acquiring a "tone" about it.

And you'll learn how to support her through the birth, mostly by getting out of the way and not forgetting to bring her "go bag" full of special stuff she wants in the room (and your kick-ass "Birth Jams" mix CD that she will *definitely* love).

MUSTACHES AND BIRTHS AROUND THE WORLD

In my birth class, we watched videos to learn about how birth differs between cultures around the world. The basics are the same everywhere: Get. Baby. Out. But attitudes and styles of birth are very different. Like, in one scene, Swedish people wandered around their Bundesmall, eating a Swedish Cinnabün minutes before giving birth.

And then there was the scene with a woman from the Amazon jungle pausing to squat and give birth while shucking some kind of weird corn. Show-off. Heck, it's enough to make you proud to be an American! People all over the world are so casual about birth; here, it's still a bit of "me time."

If you're a laffriot like me, keep your head in the game: These videos are supposed to be about the wonder of life, not about making fun of fashion disasters. Apparently, they stopped making birthing videos around 1986, so there are a lot of pastel-colored sweaters and bushy mustaches. These were some of the weirdest non-porn naked-people videos I've seen in a while, but my wife did not like me laughing at them.

Most of all, you will learn to be sappy and loving to your wife and unborn child in front of other men. There's nothing very macho about it, unless you think deep breathing and giving foot rubs is macho. But here we go: Having a kid is gonna be one big reckoning with looking uncool. Welcome aboard.

YOUR WIFE'S MOOD AND WHY YOU SHOULD SHUT UP ABOUT IT

There's no upside to talking about your wife's mood swings. That's why you should silently suffer these terrors.

Have you ever felt crazy? Yeah, well, she feels REALLY crazy.

Have you ever felt crabby? Did it make you feel better to have someone talk about it or not shut the hell up about it? Yeah, that's why you are going to shut the hell up about it.

YOU ARE STILL THE IDIOT

Your wife is changing. It's like she is a wizard now, but she's still married to the village idiot. When you approach this mighty wizard, be humble. The wizard will grow angry if you ask her stupid questions. Respect the wizard.

And this wizard is, well, a little moody. DO NOT TELL THE WIZARD SHE IS MOODY. THE WIZARD KNOWS AND DOES NOT CARE.

Unlike a wizard, a pregnant woman's powers are based in science. Hormones, discomfort, and the general problem of fitting another human in a person's body are the root of her powers.

MEN CANNOT COMPREHEND

Hormones are coursing through your wife's body in a way that us guys won't ever understand. Remember when you bit into that weird pickle right after you brushed your teeth? I'm guessing it's like that. Or maybe it's like when you sneeze and burp at the same time. See? We'll never really know.

Pregnancy is a mysterious process. It's scary, and it's weird. It's also not your body. And until future generations fix this, us men will not have to carry babies in our wombs. So maybe we stop talking about it so women don't get any big ideas. *Nothing to see here, move along....*

TAKE CARE OF THE WIZARD

Taking care of this wizard during this moody time is great prep for the moodiest of creatures: a baby.

So for now, love this wizard. Give her little foot massages, cook, and cater to this wizard. Mix the potions, vacuum, and be nice. Nobody wants to be turned into a toad.

WHAT IS A DAD NOW?

It used to be easy being a dad. You'd go to work, come home, pour a drink, and pass out by the fireplace. Every once in a while, you'd dole out advice or sign a check. From the head of the table, you'd intone on some matter of the world before drinking again and snoozing.

I've seen old Super 8 footage of the three generations of dads before me. First, my great-grandfather: unsmiling, stern, and silent. He seems unsure of whether this is to be a motion picture or a photograph, and he's pissed about it. Next, my grandfather: nice guy, but formal. One time I remember getting him loosened up was when my brother got him to listen to House of Pain's "Jump Around" on his Walkman. "Why is that guy screaming?" he asked.

Next up: my dad as a teenager about to go off to college, smiling and goofy. He's still like that. He's a warm, funny guy, but he was never a real chase-the-kids-around-the-sprinkler type; like a lot of dads of his generation, he was caught somewhere in between the strict dads of old and something new. But I give him a lot of credit for trying hard. My parents were divorced, so even driving down to get us every other weekend shows some hustle.

Each generation tries to correct the mistakes of and improve upon the previous generation—with limited success. So what about you? How will you screw up your child? Was your dad distant? Did he drink too much or have a hair-trigger temper? Did he travel too much, have crazy political opinions, or veg out in front of the TV? What can you fix?

ARE DADS JUST WORSE MOMS?

We all know what a mom is. Moms kiss the boo-boos, moms cuddle, moms hug, moms nurture. And now moms work a full-time job, cook, do laundry, and basically kick ass and take names, cranking at 110 percent all the damn time.

Is that what a dad is now? Does he kiss the boo-boos, does he cuddle, does he hug, does he nurture? He works, but does he cook, do laundry, and all that other shit, too?

Is a dad just a mom, but worse? I say nay. I say a dad is just like a mom, but BETTER.

A dad can josh you or tell you to buck up. He can give you love AND tough love. He can comfort and tell you to "walk it off."

So much is demanded of moms. They can't help but disappoint. Enter dads: If we toss around the ball a couple of times or leave work early to go to the school play, it's like we are goddamn heroes. Generations of staying remote and uninvolved have lowered the expectations for dads. Sure, that's a shitty double standard, but it's OUR shitty double standard.

WHAT KIND OF DAD DO YOU WANT TO BE?

There's never been a better, freer time to be a dad. If you can liberate yourself from the restrictions of old-school manliness and machismo, from being distant and unemotional and basically no fun, the world is open to you. It's harder, but better: If you step up, you get to experience your kid and live an open life.

But sometimes the laziness and Old Dad aloofness creeps back in; it's easier to say that you're tired when you just want to look at your phone. And it's easier to be embarrassed when your kid is crying and hand them off to mom. But you get no bonus points for that.

YOU HAVE EIGHTEEN YEARS TO GET BETTER AT IT

Let's face it: Women are magical. Us men have to work twice as hard to be as good at parenting. You're freaking out, but at least it's ok to talk about it and not just bury the fear deep in your stomach like our dads had to. You might not be a natural. You might mess up here and there, but you must do so to get better at it. You have at least ten years when your kid will listen to you, maybe even eighteen. Start stepping up now.

THE BABY GEAR INDUSTRIAL COMPLEX

To start preparing, you will need a lot of gear. But there's a lot of useless baby junk out there, and the growing Baby Gear Industrial Complex preys on your fears. *Will my daughter turn out crazy and resentful because I didn't warm her wipes? Better buy a wipe warmer, just in case.* How do you know what you'll really need?

YOU DON'T REALLY *NEED* ANYTHING

I mean, if you think about it, in some parts of the world, they just throw newborn babies in a basket or something. And when they need to nurse, they can ask any lady in the village. And they have pet tigers. I know what you're thinking: *Awesome.* Sadly, it's not our reality. For one thing, keeping a pet tiger is impractical. They shed a lot.

So how do you decide what to buy and what to skip? People have written whole boring books about what "essential" baby gear to buy. So as a cheap guy who likes awesome stuff, let me give you some pointers to consider when overpaying for baby gear.

THE NURSERY: WHERE YOUR EXQUISITE TASTE WILL REALLY SCREW YOU

Having never been on Pinterest, your kid will not care about designer baby furniture. And when she does finally have opinions, she will probably like horrible things with Dora on them. So while you are pursuing your vision-board nursery, bear in mind a few things:

★ **CRIB:** On the one hand, spending money on a crib is fine because your baby is going to be in this thing A LOT. And there are safety regulations, so you cannot build your own crib or accept some weird old crib your mom saved for you in the attic. On the other hand, some cribs are made from exquisite Bengali Bubinga wood, giant in form, huge to behold, and pricey.

★ **CHANGING TABLE:** You'll probably buy an exquisite Bengali Bubinga wood changing table to match your exquisite crib. But remember that the floor is like a giant changing table that your baby can't fall off of.

★ **CRIB MATTRESS:** Crib mattress companies are as ethical and transparent as full-size mattress companies (i.e., they are as corrupt as they come). Spend no money!

★ **DIAPER PAIL:** Beware the proprietary format of this glorified trash can. Some will only fit special, expensive bags. All promise to eliminate odors, and all break that promise.

OTHER BABY SCAMS

★ **BOTTLES:** Strong opinions reign: glass or BPA-free plastic? You better start committing to whatever the ruling bottle paradigm is. Bottles, nipples, and all the accessories are not interchangeable.

★ **INFANT CAR SEAT:** Some are very fancy, but all of them have to adhere to the federal safety regulations so you're really just deciding what kind of fabric you want to clean baby throw up off of.

★ **DIAPERS:** Diapers are a huge expense. Your baby is an alchemist, changing your gold into diapers. Try to find the cheapest diapers possible that still keep the poop inside. Break out the spreadsheet and try to avert your impending financial doom.

★ **LAYETTE:** Doesn't that sound expensive? That's the fancy word for baby clothes. Sounds like the name of a French duke who eats rare cheeses. But you'll have to buy onesies with snaps on the shoulders for your baby's big head and other stuff like that. Just remember your baby will quickly grow out of it all.

NOTES ON USEFUL THINGS

★ **STROLLER(S):** A good stroller is tailor-made to its task: will you be taking it on the subway, out for a jog, or trying to jam it in your trunk every day? That might be three different strollers. Most people end up with between three and twenty-five strollers.

★ **BABY-CARRYING THING:** Babies really, really do not like to be put down, so having a few baby-carrying things can free your hands up to eat a piece of toast or play a video game. Plus, you'll look seriously adorable when walking around town with a baby strapped to your chest.

★ **BREAST PUMP:** Just buy whatever robot your wife feels most comfortable getting intimate with and be grateful that you are not involved.

AWESOME STUFF FROM OTHER PEOPLE

People love to buy stuff for tiny babies, so you will get some awesome stuff. Annoyingly, people will continue to exercise free will/bad taste and buy stuff they *think* you will like instead of the stuff on your registry.

You'll get:

★ Baby clothes with loathsome gender-reinforcing slogans like "My Princess" or "Sports-Ball Dudes Love Guns"

★ Books that looked good because some graphic designer made a children's book once

★ Cool-looking useless crap, like baby sneakers

★ Old junk your mom saved that you don't want, like weird blankies and baby shoes from the 1930s

NAME YOUR BABY SOMETHING AWESOME

Before your baby comes, you have to think up a great name. Don't fuck this up. What's the last thing you named? Your Wi-Fi network? Your band? Better get this right: It's basically your kid's future, all wrapped up in a name. Consider what a failure Farty McHateface turned out to be.

Here are some strategies to avoid ruining your baby's future.

GIVE YOUR BABY A UNIQUE NAME

It's a cliché to want to name your child something unique. Whatever happened to Samuel or John? For hundreds of years, people named their kids based on whatever was in plain sight: Buffalo-Sitting-on-Plain or Daniel.

Then again, fear of clichés is the worst cliché of all. And when you hear a really awesome, unique name, oh man do you feel jealous. Problem is, the bar here is high, and trends are hard to predict. Is the name Beefed ahead of a trend or simply stupid? What about Beef-fed? How about Heynow or Columbo? These might be perfect, or you might find that your daughter's kindergarten class has four different girls named Cheeky.

GIVE A GIRL A BOY NAME OR A BOY A GIRL NAME

How awesome is it when you meet a girl named Frank? Or a guy named Jessica? How refreshing to free gender from the shackles of history. Wouldn't you love to have a boss named Steve who is a woman? Or a waitress named Clara who is a man? Let's get those old folks scared as hell that they don't even understand names anymore.

GIVE YOUR BABY A FAMILY NAME

For most of history, people just named babies after people they already knew. They were too busy dying from plagues to worry about shit like baby names. And there's probably some of you guys who already know that you have to name your baby Charlton Thrustington Sterling Buttermore IV or your club membership will be revoked. But this burden is a blessing in disguise. You've got a "Boring Name You Can Make into a Cool Name."

GIVE YOUR BABY A "BORING NAME YOU CAN MAKE INTO A COOL NAME"

Pick a super-boring name like a family name. Let's say John. Then watch people's eyes glaze over. "We're naming him John after his grandfather *[eyes glaze over]*, but we'll call him Jasper." *Wha-what?!* Check out the excitement! Boring names with cool nicknames are a twofer, a one-two punch of interest. It's like you're saying, "This baby can be fancy, but it can also be pretty chill." He's good for daytime but can transition to night. He's a work/play baby. John/Jasper, Christopher/Topher, Sam/Chip, Theo/"The Deuce," Patrick/Peppy. It's like a baby name mullet: business in the front, party in the rear.

GIVE YOUR BABY A YELLABLE OR EXTENDABLE NAME

Don't forget to consider the yellability of the name you choose. You'll be doing a lot of yelling at your kid. "BOB!" is a great yell. "LUCY!" is a great yell. And don't overlook names that are extendable for yelling and stern talk. Alexander is a great extension of Alex for stern talking, as in "ALEXANDER GRAHAM BELL, you did *not* just electrocute that elephant!"

FUTURE-PROOF YOUR BABY'S NAME

Think about what would make a great username or log-in. Perhaps just add a *235* to the end of a common given name like Peter and cut to the chase. "@Peter235, it's time for dinner." "@Peter235, you did *not* just electrocute that elephant!"

Emojis, numbers, and "like" symbols all have a place in the names of the future. Think outside the box or pick a box emoji, unless you like your dumb name, Larry.

WHEN TO GO TO THE HOSPITAL: NOT YET

In the movies, the woman's water breaks and she yells, "Honey, I'm having this baby NOW!" She's breathing—*whoof-whoof*—the hubby's grabbing the bag and throwing it in the car, he's backing out of the driveway, and WHOOPS—the big fucking idiot almost forgot his pregnant wife! Yipes. Back up the driveway, get the wife, and then rush to the hospital, wife goes into labor, and a montage later . . . baby time!

That's not how it usually happens, right? But you do want to get to the hospital before it's too late. Then again, your wife always likes to get to the airport like four hours ahead of time and then you just sit there glaring at the "Duty Free" sign.

The truth about when to go is somewhere in between but roughly breaks down to: *later*. Yep, later!

Most first births take forever. The contractions will start, then become more regular, and you'll call your doctors, and they'll tell you to call back in an hour. And after you wait (are they *crazy*?), you'll call again, and they'll tell you that you are still a ways off (are they *drunk*?). At that point, you'll say, "F this" and figure out how to get to the hospital.

Once there, you will wait forever. There will probably be none of that rushing around in a wheelchair and getting yelled at by the stern nurse who turns out to have a heart of gold. More like: "I guess we could watch some TV or something. . . ."

I'm not sure you can avoid getting there too early. If it's your first baby, you're probably ready to be *done* with this thing already and really, really don't want to have the baby in an Uber. But it's jarring to see the professionals totally unconcerned about your rush. Doctors and nurses are insanely blasé about this miracle they are involved in. Don't they know how much this will change your life? Sadly, it won't be the last time that people fail to make you and your child the center of attention.

IT HAPPENED TO ME: BIRTH, BORING BIRTH

I almost skipped talking about birth, but that seems wrong. It's just that it's maybe the most exciting thing that will happen to you that's actually kind of boring.

Even the most notable births are boring. Think of all the extra jazzing up they had to do for the baby Jesus: Magi, Frankenstein (do I have this right?), no room at the inn, six pipers piping, the star, etc. You won't have any of that, probably.

If you don't believe me, there are any number of parents that are happy to tell you their boring birth stories. I'd rather hear a story about the specific route someone took to my house due to traffic or a story about why the printer keeps jamming. Let me demonstrate, but please don't drive or operate heavy machinery while you read this:

OUR WONDERFUL BIRTH STORY

We rushed there, thinking my wife was about to have the baby, but we were way too early (see above) and then my wife was in a lot of pain and having contractions so I tried some half-assed massaging, but eventually they gave her some drugs. Then we watched some TV and there was more pain and medicine and a lot more pushing and my wife wasn't that into my awesome mixed CD (*crazy!*). Then there

QUIZ: SHOULD YOU HIRE A BIRTH PHOTOGRAPHER?

Many people like to hire a birth photographer to document this special day. Should you?

★ What was the last birth picture you "liked" on Instagram?

★ Does your wife prefer to look terrible in pictures?

★ What's your most private moment? Did you miss not having an audience for it?

★ Do you miss that annoying photographer from your wedding?

★ Will this be the last time you get a picture of your baby?

★ Do you have too many friends and want to alienate some?

★ Do you believe in pushing the boundaries on everything or just important things?

If you answered yes to one or more of the questions above, then you know how to take a quiz!

was more pushing and pushing, but the baby would NOT come out so it was time for a C-section (not in the birth plan!). Then holy crap: a baby!

See? Suffice it to say, birth will be intense, bizarre, and momentous. It'll be a great bonding experience for you and your wife. It'll be scary and a little boring. But then the real work begins: parenting.

DO YOU HAVE A CAR SEAT? OKAY, COOL: HERE'S A *BABY*

It's shocking how little you need to walk out of a hospital with a baby. Apparently, after all this preparation and waiting, all you need is a car seat to take a baby home. WTF.

Really. They check your wristband thing to make sure you didn't trade up for a better baby and then check that you have a car seat. Then it's "buh-bye." Good luck installing it correctly; hopefully your cabbie will help you.

PREREQUISITES FOR HAVING A BABY

There are none. Nobody asks:

- ★ What are your plans several years from now?
- ★ Have you ever held a baby for more than five minutes?
- ★ Are you ready?

Unlike getting a bank account, a YouTube log-in, or a beer, there are no prerequisites to having a baby. All you need are the necessary hardware requirements and a car seat.

PEOPLE ARE TRYING THEIR BEST, AND THEY'RE BAD AT THAT

When you think about it, it makes perfect sense, considering the terrible parents you see everywhere. Does it *seem* like other parents know what they're doing?

It's jarring. Or should I say jar-*inspirational* . . . ?

Welcome to Parental Empathy 101. Now that you are Childed, it is time for your transition from hating other parents to *feeling their pain*. It turns out most people are doing the best they can in their circumstances. In fact, probably only 40 percent of them are *actually* terrible.

So now when you see some dumbass with a kid, think a kind thought. After all, it's not his fault. All he needed was a car seat.

CHAPTER THREE

MAN ★ VS. ★ NEWBORN

KEEPING THIS WEIRD THING
ALIVE AWHILE

NEWBORNS: THIS IS GOING TO BE TOUGH

My wife and I were the first of our group of friends to have a baby. We were desperate to stay "with it," and since going out was a no-go, we had our Un-Childed friends over to watch *The Sopranos*. Just like normal! Look at us: two totally casual people, just like we were, except for this baby!

But that was when our daughter was at her most "fussy." "Fussy" is what you call a screaming newborn when it's yours. You don't call it "wailing" or "crying that will drive you insane." You call it "fussing."

Everything would start great: *What a cute baby we had!* We probably seemed like impossibly cool parents, heroic maybe: *How are they still so hip?*

But then our daughter would start crying and screaming. You know, *fussing*. My wife or I would take her to the other room to shush and rock her. But she would not be consoled. *Blam, blam!* Oh my God! Someone was being offed by Tony, but who?

Time for some real Baby Whisperer stuff: swaddling that baby up, shushing, swinging and rocking, replicating the womb, soothing her back into sleep just in time to see the end credits.

Our friends were kind, pretended not to judge, and made tracks. *"We'll never be like that, will we, honey?"* they probably said to each other as they merrily went out for a nightcap. Two years later, they were in the shit just like us.

That's what having a newborn is like: You're smiling, trying to seem awake, desperately trying to function like you are not yet a new person, hopelessly drawn away from your prior life into a Childed reality. It's just the old you plus a baby, right?

Not exactly. Newborns are tough. For now, your newborn is a human baby in name only; it is a weird ball of need, reduced to the most basic human functions:

★ Eating

★ Sleeping

★ Pooping

★ Crying

★ Wondering what the hell they have done with their lives. Oh wait, that's you.

And despite not doing anything funny and charming, this newborn demands all of your attention. It's a screeching oddity that eats and poops and keeps you awake like you're some kind of Guantanamo detainee. But the sick part is: You love it! And anyway, it's *your* screeching oddity.

And then there are the quiet moments, when this tiny thing is asleep or just *being*, and you'll feel such love for her. At moments like this, it all seems so worth it. Oh my god, she's smiling! No, wait—she's pooping.

THE FIRST FEW WEEKS OF NEWBORNS

Aren't you supposed to be taking care of a newborn baby? You don't have time to read a bunch of nonsense right now! Here's a quick rundown of what you need to know.

NEWBORNS EAT A LOT

Newborns breast-feed or drink formula. Breast-feeding is better, but this is a whole thing. Help your wife by doing bottle-feedings and being a cool guy.

NEWBORNS SLEEP A LOT

Newborns sleep a lot, but in unpredictable jags. Sometimes they even sleep while eating, which is inefficient. Basically, they're used to setting their own hours. Since you're on their time for a while, you should nap when they do.

NEWBORNS POOP A LOT

Newborns poop a lot and some of it is pretty weird looking. Time to get good at changing diapers!

NEWBORNS CRY A LOT

Newborns cry for a lot of reasons, but mostly because they are: hungry, tired, or gassy, or they have a dirty diaper—or they're bored. Or some other random reason!

WEIRDOS AND SICK PEOPLE WANT TO HOLD YOUR BABY

Don't let them. Unless they are family. Then make them wash their hands.

It's also okay to tell people they can't hold your baby. If they think you're high-maintenance, get used to it—people will be judging your parenting skills for the next eighteen years or so.

And don't make people hold your baby if they don't seem to want to. Remember when you didn't want to hold a baby?

NEWBORNS WANT TO GO BACK TO THE WOMB, BUT THAT IS NOT AN OPTION

Babies were in the womb awhile, and it was nice there: warm, sloshy-sounding, cozy, without a lot of bullshit. When you want to soothe your baby, think of replicating that nice old womb: Rock your baby gently, swaddle him up, and don't make him deal with a lot of your BS.

BURPING AND FARTING: OKAY FOR BABIES, NOT YOU

Newborns' insides are just getting sorted out, so burp your baby to release gas and disgusting, milky throw up (next time, put a baby cloth on your shoulder). Babies have a lot of gas. Sometimes, that is why they are crying. You can help by bicycling their feet; it releases gas and looks hilarious.

That's the basics for now. Close this book. Get some sleep!

WHAT'S GOOD ABOUT SLEEP DEPRIVATION?

Sleep is maybe the most beloved element of the human experience, but newborns don't know that and will keep you up all night. Sleep deprivation is maybe the hardest part of having a newborn.

But is sleep deprivation all bad? Since you won't be getting any of that sweet, sweet sleep for a while, let's pretend there's some good things about sleep deprivation.

DEEP SARCASM

Being sleep deprived can provide you with an unfamiliar deadpan delivery that will have your coworkers and friends impressed with your comedic prowess. Straight shooters will benefit the most from this change, although even the most bitterly jaded stand-up comedian can develop an extra-wry delivery with a little less sleep. Get ready to drip with sarcasm: *"I'm sooooo glad to be back at work."*

HALLUCINATIONS FOR CREATIVE THINKING

Why do people travel to the Southwest, hunker down in a sweat lodge, and take peyote when they could just have a baby? Both hallucinogens and newborn-induced sleep deprivation can cause hallucinations useful for creative thinking: *"Why don't we ship the box INSIDE the cake?"*

FALSE CONFESSIONS

False confessions are a well-known problem of torture. . . . Or should I say a well-known *opportunity* of torture? When you're sleep deprived, you can be a huge liar and get away with it. *"Yep, I am the most successful person on Earth!"*

TAKING IT EASY

Typically, much is demanded of you. Now, not so much. Sure, people will still make requests of you, but they'll know that you will fulfill them reluctantly and incompetently. Eventually, they may stop all together.

MAKING THE DREAMS STOP

At least the horrible dreams have stopped. You know, the ones you have every night where that old man keeps begging you to warn the president of impending danger? And always with the same, "Please, I've been sent to your dreams. You're my only hope and blah, blah, blah." It's like, *enough*. Or am I the only one having those?

MY APOLOGIES

There really isn't anything good about sleep deprivation. I'm sorry. I just want to tell you that you are in good company and I love you, buddy. I'm sorry you're going through this now. If you want, just skip ahead to the sleep training part. I'll try to be more helpful there.

DO YOU HAVE AN UGLY BABY?

"No?"

Okay, yes. Yes, you do.

That is a hard truth. Everyone hopes to have a cute baby, and most succeed. No one expects to have an ugly baby. But it's not all bad news:

WE NEED UGLY BABIES!

Think about it: If YOU didn't have an ugly baby, how could we tell which babies were cute? There'd be no reference point. There'd just be a wash of beautiful, cutesy-wootsy, awgoodgie-boodgie babies you just wanna EAT UP! So many cute babies. *Wook at how many!* Without your tiny horror, we wouldn't know that almost all of us have it so good.

YOUR CHILD IS ADVANCED, IN A WAY

And let's face it, almost every child disappoints. It's just that your baby has gotten a head start on it. In this way, your child is very advanced! Congratulations!

ARE SHINY, HAPPY PEOPLE SO GREAT?

Plus, there's an upside to being ugly! You can't rely on your good looks to skate by. Sure, pretty people get lots of free stuff and are loved and admired more than ugly people regardless of merit. Yes, they make more money, are selected as mates more often, have lucrative and fulfilling careers. But have you ever met a good-looking person who is happy? Okay, me too. Bad example.

UGGOS GOTTA WORK

Ugly people have to rely on their fashion senses or wits to succeed! What's that coveted skill set that everyone is so jazzed about now? No, not wealth. No, not charisma. *Persistence!* That's the one. Persistence. Persistent people succeed, overcoming obstacles. Have you ever met an ugly person who is unhappy? Me too. Maybe they weren't persistent enough. I'm trying here.

LOVE KNOWS NO BOUNDS, APPARENTLY

Doesn't this reflect well on you? Many people would be unable to love such an unlovable baby, but not you! You must be special. You must have a huge heart. It's easy to love attractive, oodgie-woodgie, cutesy babies. Be proud that you've pushed the boundaries of love so far.

A FACE MADE FOR RADIO . . . OR THE INTERNET?

For better or worse, personal charm and charisma isn't likely to be as necessary in the future. It used to be that you'd have to go into a meeting, glad-hand, and smile at people. Now you can just post something clever from your mom's basement while still in your underwear. Times have changed in the ugly baby's favor. And look how far you've come!

THE MYSTICAL CONNECTION TO YOUR BABY, LIFE, AND PRETTY MUCH THE UNIVERSE

Having a baby is a pretty profound experience. It's okay to *feel something*. I remember holding my daughter right after she was born and talking to her and realizing that she recognized me. She was reacting to my voice, familiar with me from her months in the womb.

It's kind of mind-blowing.

I mean, think about it: In a way, this little baby was created by you, and because you share DNA it's almost like she's a part of you, and you're a part of your parents, and it all goes back to some chemicals getting cooked together on a star or something, and in that way, we're all connected, right?

And I mean really think about it: This tiny person is a receptacle for all your love, so much love that you didn't even know you had, and you pour that love out and maybe that love gets secreted away into your child and is stored and then is available to love you back as this child grows, and so, in a way, we're all a giant pot of love, I guess?

And in a way, a baby is a kind of ambassador of love, sharing love with everyone, getting people talking and relating again: *Oh wow, look at that baby*, *I love you*, and *Here, take my seat, I'm getting off at the next stop*. And this little ambassador of love is just reminding people that we all love one another because we're all all-star people.

And just think about it: ESP, religion, vibes, pheromones, grooving to a song—maybe all of these are just extensions of *love*. Maybe animal instinct is just love! And because we're all animals, we just want to protect our own DNA, and I guess DNA actually stores love, and isn't that profound that we are so protective of our own love that we made dance music, I guess?

So, in a way, Babies = Love, Love = DNA, DNA = ESP, ESP = Grooving, Grooving = DJs, DJs = Babies. Or am I just sleep deprived?

HELLO, CHILDREN: I AM A NOT-AWKWARD PERSON TALKING TO YOU

Are you worried about your inability to relate to children now that you have one? Some new dads have had a lot of fun-uncle prep or big families, but some men have spent years ignoring kids.

Society is not so into grown men talking to children, especially if you own a van. But since you now have a child, it is time for you to remember how to talk to them. You can get good at this with just a little practice. Here are a few tried-and-true techniques for successfully talking to kids.

SOME KIDS WILL HATE YOU

Do babies cry when they see you? Do kids hide behind their moms when you try to talk to them?

It would be easy to write these children off as jerks, but we're trying to get better at talking to kids, not make tiny enemies, right?

Just accept that some kids will be shy or scared of you. It's nothing personal. Plenty of other kids in the sea. You shouldn't try to force the issue by yelling, "Why won't you talk to me?!"

KIDS ARE JUST LIKE SPIDERS

If you were scared of spiders, what would I tell you to do, avoid spiders forever? Never give birth to a spider? No. I'd tell you to gradually work your way up from looking at pictures of spiders to meeting a spider in person in order to get over your fear. Maybe you'd even get *too* comfortable and end up trapped in the web of a Giant Cave Spider, and then wouldn't I look foolish.

So, first of all, try talking to children. Not weirdly for no reason. But when there is a time that you might ordinarily avoid talking to kids, push yourself to say something to them. Try something banal that they can relate to. Engage!

★ **EXAMPLE:** *"What a nice train that is."*

★ **OR:** *"It looks like it might rain later."*

★ **NOT:** *"Selling undershirts is recession-proof since no one likes pit stains."*

PLAY THE BOOB

Kids love to correct grown-ups. So act like a big dummy who doesn't know anything. When they're little, it's adorable to hear their exasperation. Later, when they're teens, not so much. Enjoy messing with kids before they turn on you!

★ **EXAMPLE:** *"Your name's Aiden? That's MY NAME!"*

★ **OR:** *[Wearing hat]* *"Have you seen my hat?"*

★ **NOT:** *"Hey, you teens! Give me back my bag!"*

TALK TO THEM AS IF THEY ARE GROWN-UPS

Sometimes, it's fun to be very formal with children and treat them as if they are adults, maybe even formal British adults. Try bowing. Lay it on thick. But be careful to still talk about kid stuff, not grown-up stuff.

★ **EXAMPLE:** *"Good evening, ma'am. Have you had a nice time at the zoo today? I certainly hope the bonobo monkeys were silly enough for you."*

★ **OR:** *"I do agree; the most juiciest, yummiest juice is apple juice. Would you care for a tad more?"*

★ **NOT:** *"I heard that natural-gas subsidies are really paying off in energy independence, but who knows what damage fracking does in the long term."*

THROW IT AWAY

"Just throw it away" is an acting note I get a lot. And they aren't always talking about my headshot. It means to stop trying so hard; don't care as much. After all, most of these kids aren't going to remember you later. What, are you going to be best friends with them? You're a grown-up! Get your head in the game. This is just about practicing how to relate to children. Be okay with failing a little.

★ **EXAMPLE:** *"Off to soccer, huh? I used to play. No big deal."*

★ **OR:** *"I like your hat! This is my stop. See you later!"*

★ **NOT:** *"Is that Thomas the Tank Engine? No? Okay, I didn't even care. Whatever. Also, pretty sure that is Thomas, actually. Better look it up. Oh, that's right, you don't have an iPhone, because you're a kid."*

THE LIES OF A HAPPY COUPLE WEARING A HANDCRAFTED BABY SLING

There's something about the Mayan fabric of a handcrafted sling with a baby in it that promises redemption. Isn't it great to be a happy, baby-wearing couple?

As you step out into the street, arm in arm with your wife, a baby strapped to your chest, it's almost as though you can hear the pan flutes, so honest in their celebration of the joyful spirit of man's achievements and yet somehow still connected to this moment. You are just the latest generation to be so in love, so connected to each other and to your child and all the future that's wrapped up in him.

Of course, your mileage may vary. It's not that this feeling is a lie. Sometimes you *will* be that couple. You'll look over at your spouse and think, *Holy shit. I'm happy. I'm* so *happy.* These are times to savor, friend. You will need these times to get through the rough patches. File them away. Take pictures. Make those pictures your phone wallpaper.

But there isn't a parent alive who wouldn't admit that the first few months are incredibly hard. You're tired, you're unsure of yourself, and things are so exciting and weird and new. So give yourself a break. Don't panic. Enjoy and savor when you can; otherwise, muddle through.

Don't feel bad if every moment isn't some goddamned lovefest in which you cannot *believe* your luck. Don't feel bad if the crying and the lack of sleep and the general fucked-up baby slog you are now mired in makes you hate everyone and everything. Some days, you'll see someone out walking his dog, child in a sling, happily sipping an ice tea, and you'll want to say, "Fuck youuuuuuu."

DEVELOPMENTAL MILESTONES: WHAT'S UP WITH MY NEWBORN?

When your wife cracks out some bit of developmental trivia like, "Oh, most babies roll over by now," that's not just maternal instincts. Most women have multiple reference books, baby apps, and email newsletters feeding them developmental milestones. Should you? Probably, but she seems to have that covered.

Allow me to give you an irresponsible summary. Every baby is a little different, but roughly speaking, here's some of what your newborn will be up to.

1. **NEWBORNS DON'T KNOW THAT THEY ARE PEOPLE,** let alone whether they are cat people or dog people.

2. **NEWBORNS DON'T KNOW WHAT MAKES THEM HAPPY.** Get in line, newborns.

3. **NEWBORNS DON'T CRY TO ANNOY YOU; THAT'S THE ONLY WAY THEY CAN COMMUNICATE,** like your old roommate.

4. **EVERY NEWBORN IS DIFFERENT,** but you are not allowed to shop around.

5. **NEWBORNS LOVE FACES,** even yours, you lovable dummy.

6. **NEWBORNS SPEND A LOT OF TIME GETTING THEIR INSIDES WORKING CORRECTLY,** so you can put any kind of dumb hat on them and they probably won't notice.

CHAPTER FOUR

MAN ★ VS. ★ BABY

WHAT AN INTERESTING BABY!

INTERESTING BABY (MAYBE THE MOST INTERESTING BABY EVER?)

At some point, you may discover you have an Interesting Baby. That weird little thing is now . . . I don't know . . . FASCINATING. To you, anyway.

I have all these wonderful videos from when my daughter started to be a truly interesting baby. I have her army crawling toward a really cool rusting croquet set that we hadn't yet put safely away. I have her making crazy crooked smiles at me (now I know she was just gassy). I have her drinking a bottle in her Ramones T-shirt, *natch*.

And through it all, I have my annoying high-pitched baby talk and giggling. Each video has my adorable daughter doing something great with every mother-loving second loused up with my "aw, look at hers" and "oh hewwo, deyahs." I grate on my own nerves.

But I couldn't help myself. What a relief to finally have an interesting baby. Rolling over on her tummy, laughing, crawling: It was all so totally amazing to see someone so deeply engrossed with their own toes who wasn't my stoned college roommate.

You'll see!

When you make the goo-goo face, she says "Bawwaaaah." When you move your hand up and down, she watches it and bangs her fists! She's not just a little ball of need; she's like a traditional BABY. She's clicked in with you. She's smiling. You both are.

Think about how long it took you to learn how to use Twitter. And in the space of a few months, she's smiling, rolling over. . . . She's some kind of genius or something.

Why is the world still turning? Why are people going to work and looking at Facebook instead of just taking in this miracle? Why isn't everyone talking about "tummy time"? It's actually pretty sad how closed other people's hearts are to the wonders around them. Luckily, you know better now!

DRESSING YOUR BABY ACCORDING TO YOUR PERSONAL BRAND

Are you a punk rocker? An old-school hip-hop devotee? A sportsball fan? Great! Your baby is available to showcase your interests and be an adorable extension of your personal brand.

ARE YOU A FAN OR A SUPERFAN?

Any schmo can slap a bumper sticker on his car or tweet a link to *Deadspin*. But only parents can unleash the fearsome cuteness of their babies in service of their favorite things. Is there anything as hardcore as a baby in a Minor Threat onesie?

DRESSED-UP BABIES = SMILES

Babies dressed in grown-up clothing are hilarious. A baby cop? Who can get mad at a baby cop? If you ask me, we should only have baby cops. A baby dressed up in baby clothing is a wasted opportunity—only half as cute as he could be.

BUT IS IT OKAY TO USE MY BABY AS A PROP?

Of course! Babies can't decide about their own clothing yet. Use this special time to ascribe your own tastes to your child. Just bear in mind that it's likely—nearly certain—that your child will end up hating most of the things you love. That's parenting.

DOES A BABY WEARING A COOL THING MAKE THAT THING UNCOOL?

Probably. But bad news: You're not cool anymore! So luxuriate in this uncoolness and embrace it unironically. At least people will know you're kind of a cool parent, as cool as parents get. Which, admittedly, is not very cool.

Your *new* personal brand is Dad.

HOW TO TALK TO PEOPLE ABOUT YOUR BABY WHEN THEY DON'T WANT TO ANYMORE

You used to hate it when people went on and on about their babies, so you get it. But these dummies don't know how interesting *your* baby is. No one wanted to hear about your favorite podcast, *The Banana Brothers*, either, but now they won't stop singing the theme song. People don't always know what's good for them. How do you keep them up to date when they don't really want to be?

PRETEND TO CARE ABOUT THEIR BORING PET/ OLDER KID/BAND

Sometimes, the only way to get to talk about your baby is to listen first. You don't have to listen too much, just long enough to use whatever they say to segue into your baby talk.

Example:

THEM: *My dog's been losing a lot of weight lately, and the vet says that we need to put him on heartworm medication. . . ."*

YOU: *"Oh, my baby Stella doesn't need heartworm medication, thank God. But she's a great eater!"*

FEED THEM A "CUTE SANDWICH"

CUTE-BORING-CUTE works better than CUTE-BORING-BORING-BORING-CUTE. Offer up something cute, then something boring you want to talk about, then something cute. Before they know that they're getting a BORING, they've already swallowed the whole sandwich.

Example:

CUTE: *"Stella loves our cat Barney."*

BORING: *"I can't believe how expensive diapers are. It's almost impossible to figure out what brand is best."*

CUTE: *"She keeps grabbing her toes!"*

NO EXPLANATION, JUST START

Just start talking, launching into your story quickly so as to catch a listener off guard. Before they know why you are talking, you are done.

Example:

THEM: *"Did you say a large coffee?"*

YOU: *"Stella has the biggest poos!"*

PLAY THE "NEW DAD" CARD

Preface your story by saying how great it is to be a dad today, now that we are able to show emotion and be vulnerable; then nobody can stop you.

Example:

THEM: *"I need you to email those PDFs tonight because I have to leave early tomorrow to visit my parents in Connecticut."*

YOU: *"My dad never told me he loved me, so now I tell my baby every day."*

"ACCIDENTALLY" WEAR SOMETHING WITH BABY THROW UP ON IT

Clean clothes are for people who don't want to talk about their babies. By "accidentally" wearing a shirt with a little baby throw up on it, you're helping people remember to talk about your baby without having to make the request.

Example:

THEM: *"Hey, you have a little something on your shirt there—"*

YOU: *"That must be from Stella! I couldn't believe how silly she was being, and I guess I got a little too rambunctious with her right after she had her six o'clock bottle. You see, every night . . ."*

Soon enough, you'll be boring people with stories of your cute toddler.

BABYPROOFING: TIME TO PUT AWAY SHARP THINGS

It's very exciting to see your baby crawl and walk. Crawling, then walking, then moving away from you and never calling: That's the natural progression.

While us grown-ups always hope to sit down, lie down, nap, and then watch TV, children always want to explore. And they are especially curious about all the sharp edges and delicate things you've been accumulating in your pre-baby days. Time to babyproof.

HOW BABYPROOF MUST YOU PROOF FOR YOUR BABY?

Babyproofing depends on how crazy your kid is. My daughter weirdly never tried to turn the knobs on my stove, but nearly every other small child who came over did. My daughter *did* consistently bang her head against the sharp corner of our dining room table over and over. So, ya know, nobody's perfect.

Babyproofing is an art, not a science. You can lock up every pile of chemicals in your house, but your kid is going to find the one pile of broken glass that you leave unattended.

IS BABYPROOFING JUST CLEANING?

Your kid will want to put everything in his mouth. If you have cheap, fuzz-shedding carpets or if you routinely drop half your meal on the floor like me, some of your babyproofing will strongly resemble "cleaning." Even the cheapest slob eventually tires of constantly pulling things out of his kid's mouth and whips out the dustpan.

BABYPROOFING YOUR HOME INTO TOTAL SAFETY!

Luckily, babyproofing materials are plentiful these days. Pick a danger and the babyproofing industry has got you covered.

DANGER	BABYPROOFING SOLUTION
Pointy corners of a table	Little corner cushions
Cabinets full of poison	Cabinet latches
Very, very steep stairs leading to a rough-hewn cement floor	Baby gates
Precious collection of heavy, sharp things that you keep in the living room	Flexible plastic playpens
Top-heavy shelving unit to display your explosives	Straps to hold the shelf to the wall

Good luck getting hurt now, baby!

BABYPROOFING WILL FAIL YOU EVENTUALLY

Of course, a little common sense goes a long way. It *might* be time to store your knife collection. Babies have a way of finding the weak link in their playpens. I'm not saying don't babyproof—you must!—but it has its limits.

And you can't bundle your kid in Bubble Wrap. She has to learn to make small, nonlethal mistakes in order to learn what danger is. Better she learns about danger now, when the stakes are low, than later on, like when she marries that asshole bass player she met at Burning Man.

THE MAN WANTS YOU BACK AT WORK

Look, what do I know, I teach improv comedy. But maybe you are a responsible, bacon-bringing grown-up with a real job. In that case, the Man might be forcing you back to work already.

It's sick, right? Society tells you that dads are supposed to step it up and be more involved with family life, and when you actually *do* step it up, it's like they *swat* you down, forcing you back to work. You're supposed to be a nurturer *and* have a career? It all seems bound to lead to disappointment and guilt as we fail to achieve society's impossible demands. What are we, women?

They've had to contend with this bullshit for years. But men still get a puzzled response when they want to spend more time with their babies. People are like, "Yeah, that sounds like a good idea. . . . It's just, right now, no, no you can't do that. Because you are needed back at work."

I've heard tell that in Finland, if such a place exists, they have four years of paternity leave, six years of puberty leave, and then you are allowed to retire when you're twenty-five. Must be nice. But, sorry, here in 'merica, we've got to *work* for our smoked fish.

That said, work may be the same, but you are different.

DOES HAVING A BABY MAKE YOU BETTER AT WORK?

It's tough. Crying, huge emotional swings, late-night demands . . . but enough about your BOSS. Now that you know what love is, you also know what bullshit is. Now that you've recognized the emotional connection to your new baby, you know that "connecting" to your clients isn't that important.

On the other hand, perhaps empathy is just what work needed. Maybe *empathy* is what *synergy* means and you won't have to look that up anymore.

YOUR PRIORITIES HAVE BEEN REALIGNED

You've finally found a purpose, so who cares about work? It's not *actually* that important to wrap up the audit by the end of the month. *Not as important as a living thing, not really.* This kind of "I don't give a shit" attitude often leads to more responsibility and respect, so be careful.

Can you believe that coworkers try to describe a marketing campaign as their "baby"? Can a marketing campaign give snuggles?

YOU CAN'T DO BOTH THINGS WELL, BUT YOU CAN DO BOTH THINGS BADLY

Right now, you are the definition of half-assing it. When you're at home, you're answering emails instead of paying attention to your baby. And when you're at work, you're getting a little FaceTime with the boo-boo. Right now, that dumb guy at work is you.

But half-assing is a great way to get work taken off your plate and given to someone else. People demand too much of you, and by doing a bad job, you'll get them to stop doing that. You have but half an ass to give!

YOU ARE SLEEP-DEPRIVED, BUT THEY ARE TRUTH-DEPRIVED

Your newborn is up every two hours crying and making you sooooo tired. Lack of sleep makes you edgy, intolerant, and less polite—just what this bunch of sheeple needs to get their heads in the game. You're a truth bomb and they're a truth-bomb target. Fire away! What are they going to do? Fire a guy who just had a baby?

Oh, they will? Then start working, ya dummy.

YOU HAVE LESS FOCUS, SO LOOK AT THE BIG PICTURE

Focus is great when you want to get specific, but what about when you want to be vague and emotional? Isn't that also a valid viewpoint? It *isn't?* Fuck YOU!

Sorry about that. I'm just . . . I haven't slept.

YOU ARE A MODEL FOR GENDER EQUALITY

Women have been getting short shrift at work for decades; most companies grudgingly provide a bare minimum of maternity leave, if any. But despite the other ways we dads have benefited from the patriarchy, paternity leave is still rare. Maybe once people see how annoying it is to have you back at work, they'll push for more of it. Your incompetence might be a force for justice. Wouldn't it be great if all the annoying men at work could stay home? Then companies would really get something done!

Maybe then the "Man" will finally be a Woman.

LET'S WORK ON SLEEP TRAINING FOREVER

"Sleep training" is how you train your baby to sleep through the night without your input. If only anyone knew how to do it.

Sleeping through the night is the beginning of your steady climb back into sanity. At some point, your baby will have dropped her night feeding and will be developmentally ready to sleep through the night. And then, if you're like me, you will wait another few months until you are at full-blown crisis mode, totally off your gourd, determined to make some change that will allow you a decent night's sleep. Then you will ask: *How do we sleep train our baby?*

Scientific consensus is clear: No one can tell you what to do to achieve this noble goal. Everyone agrees that once your baby is ready, she *can* be sleep-trained. But nobody can agree on how. It's unclear what method is effective, does no lasting damage, and won't make other parents judge you when they hear about it.

There are basically three approaches to sleep training:

1. The Cry It Out Method
2. The Fading Method
3. The No-Cry Method

Full books are devoted to these methods, and God knows you would read them if you weren't so tired all the time. Here's the gist.

THE CRY AND CRY AND CRY IT OUT METHOD

In the Cry It Out Method, you mostly put your baby down to sleep and don't respond when they cry until the morning. Sleep training *done*.

★ **THE GOOD:** No one has yet to prove that leaving your baby to cry forever does lasting damage to him, and it's easy, as long as you like screaming.

★ **THE BAD:** The screaming, the horrible screaming that tears at your every fiber. Oh God, it never stops.

THE GRADUAL, NUANCED, AND HARD TO ASSESS APPROACH

Neither here, nor there, in the "Fading Method," you neither leave your child to cry it out nor respond to every cry immediately. You withdraw gradually and everything goes fine, like in Afghanistan.

★ **THE GOOD:** If you like nuance or believe in incremental change, you are gonna like this method.

★ **THE BAD:** Incremental change can feel, well, a little too incremental. Is anything actually getting better if your kid sleeps two more minutes than last month?

THE NO-CRY, NEVER LEAVE YOUR CHILD, AND THEY ARE STILL THERE NEXT TO YOU AWAKE APPROACH

The theory of the No-Cry Method is that by establishing comforting rituals around bedtime and being consistent, your child will eventually come to like sleep as much as you do. If not, your child will eventually demand you leave his room, because his college roommate is tired of you.

★ **THE GOOD:** Feels loving, easy to not feel bad about yourself for making tough choices.

★ **THE BAD:** What the fuck, aren't we trying to get sleep here? If not, let's just call it "Not Sleep Training."

HOW DO I CHOOSE?

Well, usually a friend of your wife has read a book that she really liked and that will be the end of it. Or every one of your friends will swear by the one method and act like you are screwy for asking about the other one. Or you'll try all of them in quick succession.

Like many things in parenting, it's good to have a plan, any plan. And the Having of the Plan is more important than the Plan Itself. Long-term consistency is the main thing. Sticking to your guns despite the evidence or logic is a tried-and-true aspect of being a man and should be a comfortable fit for most dads.

For our daughter, we basically chose the middle path, nuancing her into eventual sleepy submission. And now she's a ten-year-old who sleeps through the night after we read with her, give her a certain special set of stuffed animals, tuck her in just the right way, allow her to have a sip of water that she calls "glug-glug," tuck her back in, and sit with her for twenty minutes. See how easy it is?

HOW TO FOLD A STROLLER

I've seen groups of four or five adults standing around trying to figure out how to fold a stroller. The folding mechanisms on strollers are complicated, and each brand is different. Here's a handy guide.

MACLAREN

1. Kick the middle thing up.
2. Kick the side thing down.
3. Push the whole thing down until that side thing clicks.
4. Take the shit out of the bottom basket and try again.

BUGABOO

1. Pull the latch on the side.
2. Push the kicking thing off.
3. Smash.
4. Swear.

STEP AND GO™

1. *Step* on the side tab.
2. *Go* to town on the top until it folds.

UPPABABY®

1. Pull the strap toward you while pushing the bottom with your foot.
2. Foot the stepping strap.
3. Stretch the side latch.
4. Push the pulley.
5. Give uppa.

UMBRELLA STROLLERS

1. Unfold until it snaps in two.
2. Throw this away in the garbage like a broken umbrella.

TIME TO DECIDE ABOUT GOD

If you're like me, you are a semi-godless, ex-churchgoer who has fallen victim to the temptations of Sunday brunch. Or you went to church and doodled until your parents gave up on you. God just wasn't as important as sleep or not being bored.

However you forsook your God, you are now forsaken. And now here you have a tiny baby. Your religious parents want to know: Will you damn your child, too? It's time to decide about God.

IF GOD EXISTS

Let's say She does exist. Is She cool? Because if She's cool, She probably won't hold it against your child if they're not baptized or indoctrinated right away.

If God is not cool, then good luck figuring out what She wants. Opinions vary so wildly that I choose to believe that She either exists and is cool or that She does not exist. An uncool God is likely to nitpick about something you half-assed along the way. Uncool God is probably pissed I'm even talking about Her this way. She's like: "I'm a *dude*, you asshole!"

IF GOD DOES NOT EXIST

If God doesn't exist, then you are fine staying as half-assed as you've been. If you want, do some stuff to get people off your back, baptize away, knowing that a little water on a baby's head won't kill anyone. Parties and family are still important in a world without God.

DEEP INQUIRY TAKES TIME I DON'T HAVE

If you decide to do what's right, not just what's easy, then I congratulate you. Deciding what you actually believe is a tough task that I have been avoiding for years. Soul searching is hard, especially when you have a tiny baby screaming at you.

RELIGION KEEPS POPPING UP

If you decide to take this lazy path of least resistance, be warned: God doesn't go away. She keeps popping up, especially around the holidays.

And you will have to figure out what to tell your kid as they encounter more religious families or talk to their grandparents. In my household, we've had many conversations about the various religions my daughter has encountered in Brooklyn. These usually end

AWESOME, ORIGINAL IDEAS TO WIN SOCIAL MEDIA

This is perhaps your child's most "like"-able phase. Don't squander this valuable time by neglecting to post about it.

★ **THE PERFECT CUTE PIC:** Carefully pose your child to showcase the total spontaneity of your new life.

★ **DON'T OVERDO IT, BUT THEN DO OVERDO IT:** Un-Childed people can tire of your steady stream of cute pics. Take a break, get them wondering if you ever even had a kid, then flood the zone with a blast of kid pics.

★ **RIPPED FROM THE HEADLINES:** Tiny versions of famous people are hilarious—who can resist a tiny baby Senate Majority Leader or a baby disgraced former city council-member.

★ **GET REAL:** Try posting a picture of your baby in mid-scream; everyone's been there, pal. People will love your brave and honest post.

★ **TAG, YOU'RE IT:** Make sure to have people hold your baby so you can tag them. Instant "like."

★ **GET CLOSE:** Take a picture REALLY CLOSE.

★ **GO LONG:** Now back wayyyyyy up and get one of those wistful "oh look at the child all by herself" pictures.

★ **BABIES ARE A FORCE MULTIPLIER:** If you're with other babies, make sure they all get a picture together; every-one loves to see multiple babies.

after I've bored her with a too-long explanation of the Great Schism of 1054.

Or your parents may keep trying to save your child even though you are a lost cause. One Easter my daughter got a really low-budget-looking children's book in her Easter basket; it seemed to be a simple story about a rabbit, but sure enough, there was a secret Jesus twist at the end. I guess that's fair game in an Easter book.

Right now I'm still undecided on God, but my daughter is firm in her belief in the Greek Gods, having decided that Zeus and Hades are a pretty fun bunch. We'll see how serious she is when we get to the goat sacrifice.

IS IT OKAY TO BRING MY BABY TO A BAR?

Maybe no other question is so important to your sanity, you lush. It's a controversial subject. There's no clear answer and strong opinions abound.

NO: Babies in bars are annoying.
YES: More annoying than the sorority girls in the corner taking selfies? No. Anyway, bars are basically a gathering spot for annoying people.

NO: No one wants to hear a baby crying in a bar.
YES: No one wants to hear jocks chanting about a sportsball game,

but they put up with it. No one wants to hear Billy Joel on the jukebox, but they put up with it. Welcome to being outside: the land of things you don't want to hear.

NO: When I didn't have a kid, I thought it was horrible to bring a baby to a bar. Aren't I being a hypocrite if I bring my baby in now?
YES: When you didn't have a kid, you thought babies didn't belong in all sorts of places. And you thought that parents were sad losers, desperately trying to hang onto a shred of their former social lives. You were right about that, but now you are one of those losers, so fuck it!

NO: Children should not be around sin, loose behavior, and partying.
YES: Babies won't pick up a drinking habit from watching people in a bar; they'll wait for you to ruin their lives over eighteen years and then pick it up. And anyway, babies are the best partiers: They yell, shove random things in their mouths, and throw up a lot.

NO: I'd rather go to the bar without my baby.
YES: No kidding. If wishes were fishes. But by freeing your mind and allowing yourself to bring that baby around while it's still super portable, you can regain some of your lost freedom and fun. Go out, have a (slightly less exciting) blast!

NO: I don't want to be the only one with a baby in a bar.
YES: Don't worry; you won't be.

WHEN WILL MY BABY EAT FOOD?

At some point, you will introduce solid food. This is because you never see a thirty-five-year-old breast-feeding. Wouldn't that be a thing? I'd be like, "Hey, buddy, give Ma a break!"

New parents have a lot of anxiety about introducing solids, but it's really no big whoop.

Solid foods get introduced slowly, to get your baby used to the idea that food isn't always a drink. So first, you do mushy, creamy stuff. Then, when they eventually have teeth, you do more solid material. The whole thing is starting to make sense, right?

BABIES EAT BABY FOOD . . . DUH

I defer to current science to help you figure out what solids to introduce first. Back in the old days, you'd do ipecac, then straight cocaine, then Old Wives' Barley. Nowadays, it's a lot less fun: mostly rice cereal, apricots, and such. Sorry pal, I don't know what you're gonna do with all that Old Wives' Barley.

So, for a little while, baby food will seem like "baby food." Mushed-up squash, carrots, and peas; applesauce; pears; and delicious, delicious prunes. Those prunes will come in handy because your baby is going to get backed up a bit now that his food is changing. Yeah, poop will get . . . poopier.

If you've been one of those horrible parents bragging about how your baby's poo doesn't stink, get ready to eat some crow.

FOOD'S TERRIBLE JOURNEY

It can help to think of this as just a step on a food journey:

- ★ **STEP 1:** milk and formula
- ★ **STEP 2:** squishy things
- ★ **STEP 3:** mac 'n' cheese and chicken fingers
- ★ **STEP 4:** unhealthy, delicious teenage foods
- ★ **STEP 5:** unhealthy, delicious expensive brunches
- ★ **STEP 6:** healthy, repentant kale and quinoa
- ★ **STEP 7:** squishy things
- ★ **STEP 8:** the grave

But remember, there's no rush! Like many developmental milestones, you've got to keep your cool and not worry about it too much. Every baby is different (though most enjoy rattles). Some will eat solids faster than others. And don't be worried if your child never develops a taste for kale.

WHY ARE UN-CHILDED PEOPLE STARING AT ME?

As you and your baby get out and about, don't forget that there are many sad, loveless Un-Childed people whose hearts are closed off to the charms of babies. Sure, you used to be like that, but it's getting hard to remember what it was like to be so lost. If you're wondering why people are staring at you, let me remind you that Un-Childed People think that:

★ All diapers have poo in them.

★ Baby's privates should not be seen in public, even though they are just little babies and there is a diaper emergency.

★ Screaming babies and children are not "just the way things are all the time."

★ Tiny hands have filth and disease on them, transferable to everything they touch.

★ Running is an outdoor activity, not a restaurant/library/ museum/grocery store activity.

★ Pounding on things with other things is not music.

★ If a baby screams for a toy, then drops the toy, then screams for the toy, then gets the toy, then drops the toy, then perhaps the baby should not get the toy again. Maybe toy time is over.

★ Parents are Old, Sad People that they will never become.

IT'S ALL RIGHT TO CRY

Now that you're a dad, your hard heart has been opened up. Luckily, dads can cry now. They're supposed to cry. Here's a partial list of topics that will have you reaching for the tissues:

★ Phone ads and other advertising malarkey: *Maybe my cell-phone company's coverage* does *say something about my commitment to family . . .*

★ Child-in-danger programming: all those detective shows where a child is in danger that you used to not care about now make you tear up.

★ Movies about growing up like *Inside Out*: trust me, you'll be crying like a baby within minutes.

★ Really any movie or TV show with a child in it, especially when one of these things happen:

- A child loses her favorite stuffed animal, which is probably a symbol of her losing her innocence as she grows up.
- A child sleeps in her crib and parents watch lovingly nearby, but according to the trailer, they are doomed.
- A child is brave beyond her years.
- A child is wise beyond her years.
- A child teaches a simple lesson through her innocent truth-telling.
- A child just literally does anything a child does.

Doesn't it feel great to cry your head off all the damn time? What a gift!

DEVELOPMENTAL MILESTONES: WHAT'S UP WITH MY INTERESTING BABY?

* **BABY IS BEGINNING TO UNDERSTAND THE WORLD** but does not yet know about dubstep.
* **BABY MAKES EYE CONTACT WITH YOU** but no side-eye.
* **BABY IMITATES YOU** but not in a sarcastic way.
* **BABY BABBLES AND COOS** but can't yet beatbox.
* **BABY IS HAPPY TO SMILE AT STRANGERS,** even college activists with clipboards.
* **BABY BECOMES OVERSTIMULATED AND OVERWHELMED EASILY**—not very chill.
* **BABY IS STARTING TO HAVE CONTROL OVER BODY** but, sadly, cannot levitate.
* **BABY LOOKS AT HANDS AND FEET INTENTLY** but is not on shrooms.
* **BABY LIKES TO GRAB AND TOUCH THINGS** but mostly gets away with it on account of being so cute.
* **BABY FOLLOWS OBJECTS WITH EYES**—hilarious if you go around and around and around.

CHAPTER FIVE

MAN ★ VS. ★ TODDLER

WHY WON'T YOUR KID JUST BE COOL?

TODDLERS: THE SWEET-AND-SOUR SAUCE OF CHILDREN

Toddlers really mix the sweet with the sour, the hugs with the screaming. This is where the real mental work of maintaining your sanity begins. For the next few years, you're in the shit.

A toddler is like a weird little Mini-Me. He's like a real person with opinions, questions, and a personality. But also with the unstable temperament of Dr. Evil.

For one thing, toddlers can talk, but what the fuck are they talking about? It's hard to make sense of it—except that they're demanding something.

And toddlers can walk! And they can run: straight into traffic, right into the wall, and anywhere else they shouldn't.

Talking, but not. Walking, but not. Wanting, but not getting. These are the things that make toddlers so hard to deal with.

But they're also hilarious a lot of the time. And sweet. Their whack-a-doo personalities start to really become apparent. One random day, my daughter got suddenly very serious. "It's a SPECIAL day. A special day for YOU, Daddy!" she said, pointing at me. She was staring at me, very firm in her convictions, but she was a little hard to take seriously, because she was wearing a pink fuzzy hat and upside down rose-colored glasses. It wasn't a special day, but a lot of days like that feel special.

Watching your daughter sing and dance to music or ooh and ahh over something "beautiful" like a crappy drawing you made for her gets you looking at the wonder of the world again.

But how many other days did we have to endure a tantrum, a breakdown over nothing? When babies cry and go crazy, it usually means they're hungry or tired. But with toddlers, you don't always know what they want, and sometimes they don't either. All anyone knows is that the horrible dad pushing his screaming kid down the street in a stroller must be a truly stupid and bad person.

You can't avoid the world outside, though. In fact, you're probably aching to get out of the house. Be brave and hope your kid naps through most of it.

RESPECT THE NAP SCHEDULE

Nap schedules are like religious beliefs: If you pretend they're optional, you'll pay for screwing them up later. Naps are important to keep your toddler from becoming insanely cranky. It's the only time you can get anything done (like your own nap). So many things mess this up.

UN-CHILDED PEOPLE SHALL NOT MESS WITH THE NAP SCHEDULE

The nap schedule is not to be messed with. Un-Childed people will invite you to all sorts of fun activities that will fuck with your nap schedule: Brunch at 11 AM. Concert in the park at 4:00 PM. Late lunch at 2:00 PM. The Un-Childed don't understand naps. It's great to see friends, but is it great enough to justify the clusterfuck your day will become without a nap?

LIVING YOUR LIFE IN TWO-HOUR INCREMENTS

It's not like you're a prisoner, it's just that the day has a certain *rhythm* to it. It's simple! You're flexible. It's just better to see friends or do things during *free time* instead of during nap time. Here's a schedule for reference.

* **6:00–8:00 AM:** Wake up, breakfast, and playtime
* **8:00–10:00 AM: Free time**
* **10:00–11:00 AM:** Snack time
* **11:00 AM–12:00 PM:** Nap time
* **12:00–2:00 PM:** Lunch- and playtime
* **2:00–4:00 PM:** Nap time
* **4:00–5:30 PM: Free time**
* **5:30–6:30 PM:** Dinnertime
* **6:30–7:30 PM:** Bath and story time
* **7:30–8:30 PM:** Bedtime

So you are free from 8:00–10:00 AM and 4:00–5:30 PM to totally do whatever!

WHAT ELSE MIGHT SCREW UP THE NAP SCHEDULE?

It's amazing how many things can mess with the nap schedule besides the Un-Childed.

* Going to bed too late the night before
* Going to bed too early the night before
* Getting up early
* Getting up late
* Big meal
* Ride in the stroller
* Ride in the car
* Ride on the back of the bike
* Long morning nap
* Weird mood
* Yard care
* Atmospheric pressure
* It's Tuesday

- ★ UPS deliveries
- ★ Wrong number won't stop calling
- ★ Cat keeps jumping on a stack of boxes
- ★ A mirror placed at an angle reflects a beam of light into an otherwise darkened room
- ★ *New York Times* Breaking News alert on your phone even though you swear you turned those off
- ★ Passing parade of veterans celebrating Casimir Pulaski Day

DROPPING NAPS LIKE THEY'RE HOT

Eventually, most kids drop from two naps to one nap. Then from one to none. There's a transition where that later nap just doesn't seem to be sticking consistently. You'll chalk it up to a bad day and then it'll happen again.

For a little while, it will just seem like your kid is being willful. You will sometimes be able to lull them into sleep without getting so desperate that you scare them.

But it's actually them dropping their nap. It's very hard to say good-bye to that wonderful nap time. What are you supposed to do, be with your kid all day? On the plus side, you are free to try to see friends now that your life is a wreck. Better go outside.

CHANGING YOUR BABY ON THE COFFEE-SHOP COUNTER: A CASE STUDY IN THE CHILDED MENTALITY

There you are changing your baby on the coffee-shop counter when you realize: "Oh crap, I'm changing my baby on the coffee-shop counter."

Yeah, let's channel your former self for a moment and make sure you aren't the reason Un-Childed people hate all parents.

Oh, how far you've fallen. It's okay, pal, you're in the Fog of War. In parenting, moments of clarity are few and far between. You've doubled down on bad decision after bad decision; the sunk costs are high, and here you are.

AN AMAZING STORY OF WHAT MIGHT HAPPEN IF YOU START CHANGING YOUR BABY ON THE COFFEE-SHOP COUNTER

You started with noble goals. But parenting is defined by the slippery slope. A few steps later, you're a monster.

★ You're stir-crazy, aching to get out of the house.

★ You want to expose your kid to music! Kids are supposed to be exposed to music, right? So you find a sing-along to go to at the local coffee shop.

★ And then it's so fucking crowded.

★ And, who knows why, but your baby seems to love to poop on the road, much preferring to let loose when you're not at home. So you arrive with a noticeably full diaper.

★ But because every other cooped-up, overachieving parent has also brought their kid to the sing-along, the bathroom is perpetually full of nannies and moms taking their sweet-ass time.

★ And because you can't ever get anywhere on time anymore, the singer's already started with the "Itsy Bitsy Spider" shtick.

★ And it's not like you're going to go to a sing-along and not fucking *sing along*.

★ So it's easy, no big whoop, changing the baby on the counter quickly. Dads are resourceful!

That's how you ended up at a sing-along in a coffee shop, changing your baby in front of horrified hipsters, your child's ass inches away from a stack of oat currant scones. You've fallen so far.

DADDY DIAPER BAGS: 25 ESSENTIALS

A prepared dad is a happy dad! Still, what are we talking about here? There's no way you should be carrying around 25 things. I hope you know that. C'mon, man. Maybe you're a little freaked out right now, but focus. "Essentials" are an *illusion*.

And a diaper bag? Buddy. You have a diaper bag? Why? Women carry diaper bags. Unless you were somehow able to get a cool-looking diaper bag on that baby shower list, you are gonna look like a wimp walking around with that giant, girlie-man diaper bag. Put that shit in your backpack or courier bag. You've still got it! I believe in you.

Okay, great. Here we go. I don't even know if we will have a *single* essential, but let's start counting and see where we get:

1. **SUBWAY PASS (CITY FOLK ONLY)**
2. **WALLET:** for buying the stuff I won't let you pack.
3. **DIAPERS:** OR NOT. If you don't bring any diapers, it's no biggie. Most babies don't really care about clean diapers. *Parents* care about clean diapers. It's all a mind game. I'm just trying to free you up here, pal.

Done. There you go: just two things on your list. Subway pass and wallet. Or one if you don't live in a filthy city. You can buy anything else on the journey if you need to. Freedom!

But since you're carrying around that backpack, might as well put a few more things in it.

3. **DIAPERS:** Might as well.
4. **WIPES:** Okay, you do need these. Wipes are kind of the best.
5. **BOTTLES:** You damn well better have these if you have a baby. Don't be crazy.

6. **SNACKS:** Actually, fuck snacks. What were you going to do today with your kid? Didn't you plan on eating somewhere? That's like half of your day: eating stuff. So eat good stuff at a yummy restaurant somewhere instead of eating Pirate's Booty. But, then again, snacks come in handy. All right, bring them.

7. **DRINKS:** If you're bringing snacks, better bring drinks, too.

8. **PACIFIER:** Better bring that.

9. **BLANKIES:** Keep baby warm in chilly stores and on the subway.

10. **PHONE**

11. **KEYS**

12. **KID BOOK TO READ**

13. **FUNNY DAD BOOK TO READ—MIGHT I SUGGEST *MAN VS. CHILD*?**

14. **TOY**

15. **EXTRA PACIFIER**

16. **EXTRA CLOTHES**

17. **SUNSCREEN**

18. **HAT**

19. **HAND SANITIZER**

20. **DIAPER CREAM**

21. **PORTABLE CHANGING TABLE**

22. **TISSUES**

23. **BURP CLOTH**

24. **PEN AND PAPER**

25. **FIRST AID KIT:** Since you're already bringing all this other junk.

Can't you smell the sweet freedom? Now get out there, you son of a gun!

WHAT WILL TODDLERS EAT?

Food used to be one of your top five things—remember brunch?—but toddlers ruin food. You try to serve them healthy things, lovingly crafted, only to see them reject or smash them. Just a short bit ago, you were trying so damned hard to get them off the bottle, and now eating is all drama.

THEY WON'T EAT HEALTHY FOOD

When you were a kid, "food" used to mean PB&Js alternating with mac 'n' cheese and Froot Loops. Fine for you, perhaps, but for your precious child, this will not do. Now you must buy organic. Now you must pretend that grapes are dessert. Broccoli used to come with a cheese sauce. Kale wasn't even invented yet.

When thinking about food, it's good to bear in mind the big picture: You want your kid to eat. She *must* eat. And you must get her to eat, even if that means hiding something healthy under delicious cheese sometimes.

A TODDLER'S PALATE IS A MOVING TARGET

Toddlers don't want *that*. They want something else. And when they get *that*, they don't want *it*! Toddlers like a bunch of small plates: maybe a few carrots; a little pile of noodles; some kind of new, expensive organic snack. Whatever it is you think your kid likes, don't get attached—she will decide she hates it soon.

THEY WANT SNACKS

Any meal presented with enough import is likely to be rejected. Snacks are like a more casual meal. Toddlers love snacks. Since every dumb thing has to be cut up anyway, might as well get over this and accept that "snacks" are what your toddler will eat.

FOOD CAN BE FUN (SOUNDING)

Toddlers are fussy eaters. A tried-and-true method of getting your kid to eat something is to make it "fun!" That's why they are called chicken nuggets, not "chicken necks and gizzards." Get your kid to eat with some of these renamed classics.

★ **PIGS IN A BLANKET:** a hot dog in a pastry shell

★ **PIGS IN A SLEEPING BAG:** a hot dog in a slab of whatever bread you have

★ **THOMAS THE TANK ENGINE DERAILMENT:** hot dogs piled up next to mashed potatoes

★ **STONEHENGE:** hot dogs randomly strewn on a plate

★ **BIGFOOT'S LOG CABIN:** hot dogs stacked in a pile

★ **DOG FIGHT:** pile of hot dogs

★ **MONSTER BOOGERS ON A MAGIC CARPET:** Pirate's Booty on a slice of American cheese

★ **PILE OF ANTS:** raisins

★ **AMAZONIAN DEFORESTATION:** broccoli

★ **WEIRD POO:** baby carrots

★ **BABY CARROTS:** normal carrots

★ **CHICKEN NUGGETS:** chicken nuggets

★ **MASHED YUCKY DIRT SAUCE:** hummus

★ **PRINCESS TRUMPETS SUFFERING UNDER A CHEESE CURSE:** mac 'n' cheese

THEY WANT FINGER FOOD

Finger food gets picked up. Then it gets mashed and thrown. It can be horrible to witness and even more horrible to wipe off. But utensils are merely catapults for longer distance flinging.

GOD FORBID YOU ARE ALSO THE ONE
WHO PREPARES MEALS

Are you a wonderfully enlightened dad who prepares the meals? Wow, good for you. It's so great that men are sharing in what used to be "women's work." Sadly, you will also get to know the "women's heartache" of watching your lovingly prepared meals declared "yucky" and "no, NO, NO."

THE CRAPPY TRUTH ABOUT
POTTY TRAINING

If you're relying on a humor book to tell you how to potty train, then you are a braver parent than I. I'll never forgive myself for basing my daughter's sleep training on Jerry Seinfeld's *SeinLanguage*.

But I also understand that I have to say something about Potty Training, as it occupies one of the big three anxieties for new parents:

1. Sleep
2. Food
3. Poop

The truth is that potty training is even more of a goddamn mystery than sleep training. Nobody knows what the hell works; that's why you will read 459 articles about it.

OKAY, OKAY, BUT WHAT ARE THE BASICS

Basically, you wait until your kid is old enough, then you encourage her to use the potty. If you try too early, your kid won't be able to do it, and since she's become so accustomed to sloshing around in her own poopie, she'll need some guidance to understand the benefits of toilets.

So you buy a funny little potty to put next to the real potty and you get her psyched about it: "What a cool place to take a shit! Your own Dora potty!"

Then you see if she wants to try it out sometime: "What do you think? You want to try being a big girl and pooping in the Dora potty?"

Then, if she does, you make a big deal about it: "Wow! Look at that! You pooped in the potty! Holy shit that's great!"

Over time, you encourage her by taking her out of diapers and getting her to use the potty. She starts to pay attention to when she has to "go potty" and thus begins your life of "accidents."

THIS SOUNDS LIKE IT TAKES A WHILE

Yes and no. It might, or it might not. That's the main problem. Every kid is different, and just like with sleeping, eating, and every other damn thing, your mileage may vary. Like I said, you'll want to read up on this. When I was trying to potty train our daughter, I read something about "Potty Training in One Weekend," but I see now that there are wild promises of potty training in less time. Give one of them a try!

WHAT ABOUT ELIMINATION COMMUNICATION?

Elimination communication is the idea that infants give cues to their parents when they have to poop and pee, allowing parents to never have to diaper their kids. Hey, good luck with that. I have enough problems without having to explain why my baby is peeing in someone's sink.

THE BOTTOM LINE

Get it? Anyway, potty training eventually works. I've only met a few grown-ups wearing diapers, and they were nearly all alternative comedians doing late-night comedy shows.

IT HAPPENED TO ME: I WAS THE DAD IN A MOMMY GROUP

If you're a stay-at-home dad, it's time to admit that you need to talk to other grown-ups. Women have created a solution to this problem: the "mommy group." These are groups of moms who have come together to lend one another support, have some fun, and socialize their children. Some may call themselves "playgroups." And yes, they are basically all women.

When I first joined my mommy group, it was at the invitation of a mom I met at the playground with her kid. She said, "Hey, there's a mom's group that gets together sometimes, if you're interested. Sometimes, there's even a dad there!" This was basically a kind lie, and if I wasn't so desperate for normal human conversation, I might have passed on the opportunity. But at this point, I was stir-crazy, tired of being at home, and ready to force myself to socialize. I thought to myself: *This could be fun. And my child probably needs to meet and hang out with other kids. And sometimes, there's a dad there.* You could smell my desperation.

One of the first times I went to the mommy group, I almost blew it. I had my daughter in her stroller and was hustling off to the home of one of the moms I hadn't met yet. I was trying to arrive casually late so as to not appear too stuffy or eager. *See, I just come when I can! I'm a totally cool guy. I'm just totally whatever about everything!* We found the place and I rang the bell. Just then, I looked down and realized that my daughter had fallen asleep. Now I was squarely in creep territory. What kind of a weirdo brings a sleeping kid to a play-date? Seems *pretty* desperate. Luckily, I was able to shake her awake before the mom showed up at the door. We were invited in, and my groggy child played near the mom's child while the grown-ups chatted. Success! I'm not a creep!

There are probably different ways mommy groups work, but in mine, we'd meet once a week at someone's apartment or, if the weather was good, in the park. What this meant was that six or seven women (and me) would bring their kids and let them go nuts on someone's home. We'd eat a little something, maybe have some beverages, but it was always somewhat short of what you'd describe as a "party." And because toddlers don't really give a shit about other people, it was basically a few hours of managing stolen toys and meltdowns with a little grown-up talk interspersed throughout. And that was enough!

GOOD THINGS ABOUT BEING IN A MOMMY GROUP

★ Grown-ups speak and don't throw things.

★ Neglecting your kid near other kids is called "parallel play" at a mommy group.

★ They're great practice for making friends (for you, that is).

★ They're a good place to compare your kid to others and reassure yourself that your toddler is less of a dick than some other kids.

★ They're a great way to see if other people's apartments are as trashed as yours.

WARNING FOR DADS!

You CANNOT be weird. Now is not the time to tell these moms about the slogan you came up with that doesn't have a product yet

("The ooze you can use!"). Now is not the time to talk about your video games or your other dumb geek shit. Stow it. Even the smallest whiff of "weird guy in a bunch of ladies" is enough to break the spell and get you removed from the email list.

TANTRUMS: WELCOME TO THE DARKNESS

The main thing about toddlers isn't toddles, it's tantrums. I guess "tantrumers" doesn't roll off the tongue sufficiently. Tantrums are the ubiquitous freak-outs wielded by toddlers everywhere to get what they want through a combination of embarrassment and torture.

EVERYONE THINKS YOU ARE A MONSTER

Most parents will do almost anything to make tantrums stop. Private, home-based tantrums are horrible, but they are manageable for strong parents. But what do you do about public tantrums? Everyone stands around staring, watching you fail, and blaming you for the screaming child ruining their day. Tantrums aren't your fault!

Of course, maybe you forgot to feed your child. Or you skipped a nap in violation of the sleep schedule. You did both? Wow.

But embarrassment is the enemy of good parenting. A parent impervious to embarrassment is an irresistible force.

EVERYONE THINKS DADS ARE DUMB

For centuries, men have reaped the benefits of male privilege: first dibs in land, voting, power, etc. But mid-meltdown, that power dissolves and the centuries of female wisdom and child-rearing responsibility comes back to haunt the beleaguered dad.

Nosy biddies all over will start to question even the best dad if he is with a kid in mid meltdown. They just assume that you are as big an idiot as all the lovable TV dads they've come to know from the story box they watch at home, and they will give you some "extra help." Try to accept this help as graciously as possible.

They'll say, "She looks hungry!" or "Is everything okay?" If you get sarcastic or angry, all you've done is confirmed that you are a big dumb dad who doesn't know how to keep it together. Give them a politely clenched smile like mothers everywhere have practiced forever.

TALK TO YOUR KID LIKE SHE IS A TINY CAVEMEN

Although some tantrums are inevitable, many are caused by the frustration a toddler has in communicating her desires and feeling heard. There's lots of advice out there on this. One approach I enjoyed came from the book *The Happiest Toddler on the Block*. This book advised that toddlers are like tiny cavemen—and not just because they both wear overalls.

According to this view, the correct approach can mitigate tantrums.

1. It's best to talk to toddlers in short, emotive phrases, as if you are talking to a caveman. But instead of saying things like "Big sky-bird eat mommy" (*Caveman*), you say things like "You want snack! You want SNACK! You hungry! SO hungry!" (*Toddler*) to mirror their concerns back to them in a way they'll understand.

2. Then you add what you want to get across: "But daddy no have a snack! Snack when we home. Almost home. Then SNACK!" The book calls this the "Fast-Food Rule"—somewhat confusingly since now I'm just thinking of that drive-in on *The Flintstones*. It's called this to help you remember to repeat back "his order" (what he wants) before you tell him "your price" (what you want).

3. I also think it's fun to say "May I take your order?" but your mileage may vary.

If talking like a caveman doesn't work, you can always try an old dad standby: ignoring. Most dads are great at ignoring things, a handy characteristic when a kid is pitching a fit in public and can't be reasoned with. Know that you are not a bad dad, despite what *literally* everyone else in the world thinks.

CLASSES FOR LEARNING AND SANITY

If you're a stay-at-home-dad, or even just a guy whose wife tells him to fuck off and leave the house with his kid on Saturday mornings, you might be in the market for classes and activities. When I was a kid, you were lucky to get story time at the library with some old librarian who wouldn't even do the voices. I'm looking at you, Ms. Randall.

Nowadays, there are so many options. I'm literally looking at a webpage that lists "101 Classes for Kids in Brooklyn."

★ Abracadabra Magic Club
★ Art for Tiny Picassos
★ Art for Tiny Rembrandts
★ Art Without Borders
★ Baking Without Pans
★ Ballet Buddies
★ Bilingual Baking
★ Brooklyn Botanic Garden Explorers
★ Brooklyn Crafts
★ Brooklyn Dance for Tiny Picassos
★ Creative Artistes
★ Baby Batali's Pasta Making
★ Baby Soul Cycle
★ Coding for Cuties
★ Dance and Dough
★ Everyone Gets a Trophy
★ Extreme Kids
★ Etc.

Pretty much everything but investment banking, which is a shame; I ain't enjoying my golden years on my daughter's hip-hop dancing money.

WHY? WHY WOULD I DO THIS?

Classes and activities are there to get you out of the house and provide a little fun and structure to your day. Sometimes, you just need to talk to other grown-ups—or at least talk *near* other grown-ups.

Also, your kid might like it.

WILL MY CHILD REALLY LEARN FRENCH?

No. Usually these classes are like a Learning Annex version of a real class, but for kids. So in French class, you say "*Oui*" and pretend to mime boxes. Maybe you roll a tricolor ball around and have croissants for a snack. In circus class, you tumble around and do face painting. Then you roll around a circus ball and have peanuts for a snack. Filmmaking is yelling "action," tossing a ball, and having popcorn for a snack. Basically every class is themed ball rolling and a snack.

WILL I MAKE FRIENDS?

Maybe. Some classes are full of moms and nannies and you must be on your best behavior to not be the "weird dad." Other classes might have more dads. If you can get past the natural big-dog distrust and competition between men afraid to seem vulnerable because of a sad legacy of American macho behavior and failure to nourish the feminine side, sure, you might make a friend.

JUST DO THE DUMB THING

If you're supposed to "walk like an elephant" or do some silly nonsense with your kid, go ahead and do it. There's nothing worse than someone who is being too cool for school, especially when that school is a music class for toddlers. Embrace the experience and enjoy yourself. Be goofy. I think the only way we get dads to be truly accepted as caregivers is to seem pathetically vulnerable. Give it a try!

TIPS

★ Don't screw up the sleep schedule. There's nothing quite as wasteful as a kid who sleeps through his class.

★ Don't worry about people judging you (they are actually judging your kid).

★ Winter classes are good for getting out of the house, but bear in mind that the first twenty minutes and the last twenty minutes of every class will be devoted to taking off/putting on coats and getting kids out of/into strollers. That leaves only five minutes for ball rolling and snacks.

WHY IS MY KID A SHITTY ARTIST WHEN I AM SO CREATIVE?

It's not that you don't love your kid. You do. But his scribbles . . . fail to show promise. Or maybe your daughter seems to screech her way through "Wheels on the Bus." Has the apple fallen so far from the tree as to be more of a pear than an apple? Does your kid kind of suck at art?

IT'S JUST THE EARLY DAYS

Hey, it's way too soon to worry about this. Your kid is just learning to draw. He picked up walking pretty quickly! Plus, it's like they say:

practice, practice, practice. This kid has to explore, do shitty rough drafts, and make mistakes. Just maybe not quite so many mistakes.

MAYBE HE HAS NOT FOUND HIS MEDIUM

Who can predict the manner in which the Muses kiss one's brow? Your son seems to like kicking balls; maybe he is a dancer! Also, he likes to break things; maybe mixed-media montage or large-scale found object assemblage is more his oeuvre. When he yells, "No more art! I hate art!" and cries as he flings his paintbrush from the table is that a nascent Oscar-winning performance?

MAYBE YOU ARE TOO CLOSE TO THE PROCESS

As a parent, you are your child's most important artistic mentor. Because you collaborate in her work by cutting out shapes or mixing paints, you might be too close to the process to judge it fairly. Maybe the work is better than you think; perhaps you need to share your child's work more widely to ensure that it finds its audience. 'Gram that shit.

MAYBE *YOU* ARE NOT A GOOD ARTIST

Is it possible that your child *is* as good an artist as you are because you are a terrible artist? If that's true, perhaps the art world is bullshit and you and your kid are on the vanguard of *rethinking art itself.*

HIGH-HANGING FRUIT

And then again, if everything came naturally, if there was no struggle, would the world be better for it? No. Struggle is what defines value; low-hanging fruit isn't the best fruit. High-hanging fruit is! You have to climb trees or get a big ladder to get high-hanging fruit. Maybe you need to eat a lot of low-hanging fruit to understand how gross it is. Maybe that's what motivates you to build the ladder in the first place! And then maybe you become a ladder builder instead of a fruit picker. Exactly.

QUIZ: IS MY CHILD TOO ANNOYING FOR THIS RESTAURANT?

Short answer: YES.

Some baby-hating snobs will complain if even the most minor of baby noises has sullied their freewheeling evening. On the flip side, some parents act like we're all part of their babysitting co-op. So how do you know if you're one of the good guys or if you're just desperate to eat out like a person again?

Here's a handy test to tell if your kid is actually too annoying for a restaurant:

1. If you did not have a special fondness for the child in question, would you have a special hatred for him?
2. If a grown man was doing what your child is doing, would that be okay?
3. Is the volume on your child's iPhone game/video turned on?
4. Could your child be described as having "done laps" around the place?
5. Have you noticed that your child is dining with you? If not, where'd he go?
6. Is the average star count in the restaurant's review higher than the age of the child?
7. Do you keep trying to get some other table involved in what your kid is doing like everyone in the restaurant is all part of some big baby party? *"Eric's saying hi to you! He's three!"*
8. Has a toy been thrown? Has it been thrown a few times?
9. Is your kid hiding under the table?
10. Is your kid screaming?

If you answered yes to four or more of the above questions, you are really taking this quiz thing seriously! And yeah, your kid is crazy annoying. Go home!

KIDS' MUSIC IS BAD AND IT ONLY COMES IN THREE VARIETIES

Before you're a parent, you'd never guess that there is so much *singing*. But between music classes, sing-alongs, and constantly trying to inject joy into every moment of your kids' life, you're going to hear a lot of horrible, horrible kids' music.

And sadly, it only comes in three varieties:

1.   WEIRD OLD CLASSICS

Gather any group of small children, nannies, and parents and start singing, "The wheels on the bus go . . ." and everyone loses their minds like it's "Born in the U.S.A." at a Springsteen show. Everybody knows "Wheels." All the old classics are still in rotation: "Twinkle, Twinkle Little Star," "A-B-C-D," and that tribute to head injuries and bad parenting, "Five Little Monkeys Jumping on the Bed."

2.   WORLD MUSIC OF THE TIKKI TIKKI TEMBO STYLE:

The hippies of Music Together have reached into every corner of the globe to bring multicultural dreck to every child's house. Enjoy the impossible-to-follow rhythm of a traditional Kenyan counting song now that the European hegemony over kids' music has finally been broken.

3.   FAKE GOOD MUSIC:

It sounds like the Ramones "Beat on the Brat," but instead it's "Cheese on the Cat." Fake good music is the most insidious kids' music around. It sounds like good music, but it's been sanitized for children. Nothing marks your descent into uncoolness as clearly. Pretty soon, you're accidentally jamming out to "Welcome to the Jungle Gym."

CAN I LISTEN TO GOOD MUSIC?

Sure, it's just a bit trickier. Just be careful not to play anything that is too "scary." Kids scare so easily that you have to ease them into some of the deeper cuts. Wilco probably won't get your kid upset, but the Pixies are tricky. *"Daddy! Why is the monkey going to heaven?!"*

HELP, I THINK I LIKE KIDS' MUSIC

Every grown-up feels the shame of accidentally humming Laurie Berkner's "Pig on Her Head" to themselves on the subway. And there's no way you won't sing "Taxi, taxi, riding in the backseat" when you're actually in a taxi. Those are givens. Or if you find yourself at some horrible children's music concert with kids rocking out all around you, please don't cross your arms and be a buzzkill. Go ahead and dance!

This softening of all your hard edges is part of growing up, being a dad, and becoming hopelessly out of touch.

WHY WON'T THIS TINY PERSON JUST BE COOL?

You did all this cool stuff: You went to the playground and made sure your kid didn't fall off the jungle gym where that gap is way too big. You pushed her on the swing, even doing the extra "run under the swing" trick to amuse her. Then, ice cream. And not some freezer-burned sno-cone from the bottom of the bodega freezer. No, you got the good stuff: strawberry ice cream with real strawberries in it (you even picked them out for her because they were "too icy").

Sounds like an awesome day. Sounds like a twenty-hug, "I love you, Daddy" kind of a day. But now you're in Blue Bottle trying to get a fancy coffee and your kid is freaking out. That's a five-dollar rosemary olive-oil cookie she just smashed!

Why won't this tiny person be cool?

TODDLERS CAN'T BE COOL

Think about the brainpower of toddlers. They are not yet smart. They want and want. They are ruled by emotions. Their very nature is the definition of uncool: needy, stupid, and full of drama.

That's the major problem with toddlers: They don't know how to be cool when you need them to be. They can be a lot of fun one second and then suddenly become major jerks the next. They're like your sketchiest friend who hooks you up with last-minute tickets to Tame Impala but always stiffs you on the tip at Peter McManus.

BUT CAN'T THEY BE COOL FOR A MINUTE?

You'll get nothing and like it. Sad to say, but parenting is not a quid-pro-quo proposition. There's no "you do one cool thing, and they do a cool thing." Kids take your cool things for granted entirely. Yes, you will be penalized for fucking things up. No, you will not get credit for getting things right. Think of all the stuff your parents did for you. Have you thanked them? See?

With toddlers, there are just Things They Like and Things They Don't Like. Empathy isn't something toddlers learn until they are five or six or thirty-seven.

BUT I DID SO MANY COOL THINGS

I know! I'm with you, pal. I'm so sorry! Your kid is being a punk, but that might actually be your fault! You might have overdone it! Maybe you set yourself up for failure here by cramming too much into a day.

Here's where dads mess up: Guys love to multitask and optimize and bang out a day. Take advantage of the fact that your toddler is slow as hell and let the meandering *to* the playground be half the day, then *being at* the playground the other half. Toddlers like to look at the gum wrapper on the ground, point out a stray cat, touch a sharp thing. They like to take their time. Slow down and enjoy this glacial pace.

GOOD THINGS ARE NOT FOR YOU NOW

Maybe you've reached too high! I love me some Blue Bottle. Look, I'll admit that I'm pretty douchey when it comes to fancy coffee. And pre-baby, I loathed a coffee shop with a play kitchen in the back. But guess what: Those are for you now! Maybe hit a coffee shop that has one of those child-friendly areas where other grubby kids have schmutzed up the fake kitchen already. Or even a place with a picked-over stack of coverless board books. Try one of those places.

MAYBE YOU CARE TOO MUCH

Can't I just do what grown-ups do? I really want to. Yes, you can. Your problem may just be that you simply care too much. You're too good a person. Stop caring that you are ruining everyone else's good time. You're the guy with the loud kid now. Enjoy it!

But if that is too hard, no, you can't do what grown-ups do. Not now. Accept your fate.

SCREEN TIME IS A WONDERFUL TIME

Experts recommend no screen time for children under the age of two. And older children shouldn't spend more than one to two hours a day using screens. Okay, good to know.

But you were brought up on crappy TV, so a little TV couldn't hurt, right? You watched truly horrible things on TV for hours without anyone even telling you not to. And anyway, sometimes you have to cook dinner or chill out!

Practically everyone lets his kid watch some TV or play on his phone. The key is to be mindful of the recommendations you are ignoring. Limit consumption. Set firm boundaries. Encourage reading and outdoor play. Most of the time.

PHASING IN YOUR SCREEN TIME

By phasing in your child's screen time as they get older, you can ensure they have plenty of time for reading and play.

* ★ **0-2 YEARS OLD:** No TV. Okay, a little while you are cooking or on the phone.
* ★ **2-3 YEARS OLD:** A little TV when daddy needs a break. And when it's insanely cold or rainy out.
* ★ **3-6 YEARS OLD:** Special morning and evening TV and computer time and when you're cooking, on the phone, need a break, or it's raining. Or if it's super cold out. Or it's *one of those days*.
* ★ **6-8 YEARS OLD:** At this point, you and your child will have formalized whatever weird screen-time bargain you've accidentally arrived at. The rules are now firmly in place, and your kid will jealously guard his time, so good luck getting rid of it. But adding time is always an option! Especially if you have to cook, talk, think for a goddamn minute, do something, or if you need a break or if it is cold and rainy, or very hot out.

TELEVISION IS BETTER THAN EVER

When I was a kid, I watched a show, literally called *Rubik, the Amazing Cube*, about a Rubik's Cube. At least shows pretend to be educational now. And there's more racial diversity. When I was a kid, the only people of color were the Pink Panther and the Great Gazoo.

AND THERE ARE SO MANY SCREENS!

In the bad old days of one screen, you used to all have to crowd around one TV. Remember how mad you were when dad took over the TV for the afternoon to watch sportsball right when you were going to watch *Creature Double Feature*? Now that you can watch shows on your phone, your kid can have their Nick Jr. binge while you catch *The Walking Dead*. Isn't it a wholesome picture: the entire family sitting around in the living room, everyone watching their own device?

Screen time can really bring the family together. Let's face it.

PRINCESSES AND TRAINS ARE *THE MAN*

Look, you watch *Transparent*, you bake, and you diaper. You're not some knuckle-dragging, heteronormative, gender-role enforcing Old Dad; you're a New Dad. If the boy wants to wear a dress, you know it won't make him gay and you'd love him if he was. You're giving your daughter a handsaw, teaching her how to throw a ball, and setting her up to be a powerful woman.

But what the hell is it about boys and trains? And what can you do when your daughter won't stop talking about princesses? It's spooky, but there is some weird attachment to these old tropes. If your boy likes trains, should you try to discourage that?

Do princesses and trains oppress children? Are they *the Man*?

THE CASE AGAINST TRAINS

Doesn't he see that trains are part of the rigid power structure, the dehumanizing machine over man? They're a strong leader, a fixed hierarchy, and a way of thinking at odds with the fluid way our world now operates. *There's no one track, kid! Your options are wide open.*

On the other hand, is there anything wrong with leadership? Strength, fitness, THE PHYSICAL, an honest day's work, tangible progress? It sure beats blogging or creating "viral content." Maybe getting the trains to run on time is still valuable, still speaks to a time when America DID THINGS. Action over inaction! Deeds over chatter.

THE CASE AGAINST PRINCESSES

Princesses? Yuck. How outdated. Valuing beauty over skill, waiting to be rescued and validated by some MAN? Locked in a tower like some possession? Long, fancy dresses and horsies?

On the other hand, aren't we always seeking to teach children about the beauty in things? Some things are beautiful, not just in an inner way, but in an outer way, too! Nothing wrong with looking good. God bless, but it's not like people are attracted to slobs. And maybe a strong woman can recontextualize the "save me" ethos of princesses from WITHIN. Think about *Frozen*! "Let it go, let it go!"

YES, THEY ARE THE MAN

Anyway, to thine own self be true, right?

Kids never do exactly what their parents want. Most of us went through some weird phase like believing in ghosts or wearing that one AC/DC T-shirt every day. Kids grow out of these things. Try not to worry about it. I've never seen a grown-up princess, let alone a grown-up train.

WHO IS WORSE: FRANKLIN OR CAILLOU?

You ignored all the advice about not letting your kid watch TV until they're twenty, and now you have to deal with the horrible bunch of characters that louse up your kid's TV shows. Whatever happened to classics like G.I. Joe or the Herculoids? These new characters are the worst.

★ **DORA:** It's not just that she shout-talks all the time and repeats the same shit over and over, it's that she's the queen of awkward pauses. Why do you keep asking us questions, Dora? Stop seeking our approval. Just do your thing.

★ **SWIPER:** If you're gonna go swipe shit, just do it, Swiper. Why do you stop when we tell you to? When a bunch of kids yell at me to stop doing something, it basically just eggs me on.

★ **CAILLOU:** Everyone is easy on Caillou at first because they think he's cancer-ridden. Turns out he's bald for no reason! Then why is he such a creepy whiner? Why does he say his name forty times in his theme song?

★ **FRANKLIN:** Why is Franklin so worried about everything? He's a turtle and could just curl up. If I had a shell, I'd spend half my day in there texting.

★ **THOMAS THE TANK ENGINE:** I have a daughter, so honestly, I couldn't even watch ten minutes of this crap before I had to change the channel. Seems like it's classist, though.

★ **BOTH MAX AND RUBY:** Ruby is a nag, but it's almost like Max is brain damaged. He can't seem to listen to ANYTHING Ruby says.

★ **ANYONE ON *YO GABBA GABBA!*:** Seems like a cool kid's show, but fails the crucial "Can I ignore it?" test.

★ *PAW PATROL:* Rocky the Recycling Pup? Out of a handful of dogs, one of their powers is to basically put trash in the right place.

★ **DANIEL TIGER:** People give Daniel a pass because he's in the "Mr. Rogers's Universe," as if he had anything to say about it. Meanwhile, it's Daniel's fault that you're accidentally singing "When you have to go potty, stop and go right away, flush and wash and be on your way" while you're trying to take a dump.

Whatever horror you are currently suffering with, be thankful that your child is still watching TV, not just YouTube where it's hard to understate how bad the offerings are. Some parents find their two-year-olds addicted to popular videos of grown adults pretending to make their dolls talk or toy unboxing videos. Makes you look forward to a little Shimmer and Shine.

IT HAPPENED TO ME: "KINDERFREUDE"

One of the weirder things about becoming a parent is that your emotions get recalibrated in unpredictable ways. Things that you used to find cloying, you find cute. *Oh man, that kid in the YouTube video has an insane laugh!* Maybe you even start to enjoy pictures of other people's children clogging up your newsfeed. You cry during tampon commercials, right? No? *Just kidding.*

In some ways, this is just step eight in the well-trod journey to becoming uncool. Nothing new there. But there is one emotion that is new and, I think, not remarked upon enough: *Kinderfreude.*

That's probably terrible German. Like *Schadenfreude* (the pleasure one feels at another's pain), but a little different. Basically, since becoming a parent, I take pleasure in watching other parents struggle with crying children. *Kinderfreude.*

I don't know if I should feel bad about it; I'm just being honest. It's a sort of sympathy, sort of amusement, sort of *hahaha*. It's all mixed up. It's a little bit of "Aw, man, I've been there."

But I remember when I didn't have a kid, there was really only one way I felt about a crying, agitated child and his parent: "Please, for the love of God, shut up and get off this train." Now it's more complex. It's like a weird Japanese candy: sweet *and* sour.

An example: One time, I was on the train near two dads and their kids when one of the kids suddenly threw up. People around me quickly moved out of the way, one kindly person gave them a huge stack of paper towels ("Work doesn't need all these paper towels like I do!"), and I just sat there grinning like a creep, thinking "Aw, man, sucks to be that guy!" *Kinderfreude.*

GRANDPARENTS: WEIRD BABYSITTERS

It's a miracle you are alive. Growing up, after eating a bowl of Fruity Pebbles in front of *What's New, Mr. Magoo?*, you sat in the back of the station wagon, no seat belt, on your way to the backyard fireworks and gun-shooting party. None of this would pass muster these days. Is muster even legal anymore? But this is what "parenting" was back then: eat what you want, watch what you want, go outside and play, walk it off. Times were different.

So I guess it's okay to let your parents, now much older and feebler, take care of your precious child. They keep leftovers in the fridge way too long and it's been decades since they took care of anything, but it's fine!

Remember your own grandparents? Didn't they spoil you and let you watch weird TV and criticize your looks and choices? Sure they did, but you didn't question it. That's what grandparents are: weird, near strangers that you have to let be a part of your life. Seems dangerous, but if you bear a few things in mind, all will be fine.

YOU REALLY AREN'T DEAD

You're not! I know reading this book might *feel like heaven—* *wink*—but you are very much alive here on Earth. Most grandparents have retained the bare minimum understanding of what it means to keep a child alive. You were fine, you are fine, your child will be fine. Love will keep your child alive, probably.

NOBODY CARES ABOUT YOUR PLAN, ESPECIALLY GRANDPARENTS

You and your wife may have a careful no-sugar rule, careful screen-time restrictions, and a flexible, but really not flexible, sleep schedule that ensures that your child will have a healthy, happy, optimized childhood. But grandparents DGAF about that. Nobody does. Even babysitters you're paying will ignore you half the time. Your kid will be introduced to sugar by your parents, to *Minecraft* by a classmate, and to cigarettes by some smooth-talking grifter. Just strap in and release control.

GRANDPARENTS ARE LIKE SUBSTITUTE TEACHERS

You've laid out a careful lesson plan and then when you leave the room, they're like, "All right, everybody, I'm going to take a nap. Open reading period." Grandparents are just one of many groups of irresponsible grown-ups who will take charge of your children.

BEWARE THEIR WEIRD OLD-WORLD ADVICE

Whatever you do, take any advice from a grandparent with a substantial grain of salt. Some grandparents are wise baby whisperers, warm and connected to children in a special way. Others are relying on a mix of distant memories of your upbringing and *Dear Abby* columns they clipped from the local paper to give you advice.

In the end, grandparents are a combination of basically everything you would disqualify a normal babysitter for. But they are maybe the only people that love your child as much as you do. Be kind to these strange, wonderful people.

MAKING FRIENDS WITH OTHER PARENTS ON THE PLAYGROUND: DO I HAVE TO?

"Share."

"Be nice."

"Make friends."

This advice is fine for toddlers but a drag for dads. At some point, you will find yourself trying to decide whether to "make friends" with other dads at the neighborhood playground. The answer seems to be "yes," but let's make sure.

NON-STRANGER DANGER

I grew up in a small suburban town where strangers wave at you from passing cars as if to prove how friendly they are. Now that I am a jaded New Yorker, this custom strikes me as odd. When this happens to me, I think, *Do I know that person? Why are they taking up my time and making me angry?*

In New York, you always have to be careful about whom you decide to know. It's great to have friends, but anonymity is also key. One time a girl I knew from college moved to my neighborhood and I'd see her at my subway stop every morning. After months of having to say hi to each other, we both finally decided to pretend we didn't know each other anymore. Phew, back to the crossword puzzle!

So the other parents at the playground present a dilemma: How well should you know them?

MAKING FRIENDS WITH OTHER PARENTS: SHOULD I?

ON THE ONE HAND	ON THE OTHER
There might be some nice people. You could make a new friend!	If you don't hit it off, they're just a few more people you have to nod at and acknowledge, maybe even pretend to like.
You won't feel as alone in this world.	Not feeling alone in the world is what your phone is for. So you already have that covered.
Your kid might make friends.	If your kid makes friends, you'll have to get to know the parent. What if your kid is better at making friends than you?

MAN TROUBLE

This is also where being a guy is tough. I think women have an easier time being friendly with one another. Men still have a stupid macho formality we have to overcome each time we meet someone, a sort of standoffishness that's even sillier when you're holding a lovey or playing monster on the playground.

I remember going to story time at the local library with my daughter and how excited I was to see another dad there. *All right, now we're talkin'!* So right after, I introduced myself to him and he gave me a cursory nod before blowing me off for a mom he knew. Yeah, it stung. *The one that got away . . .*

DON'T SCARE HIM OFF

Maybe the proper answer is to let the familiarity sink in over time until it seems insane not to say hi. Something like this:

★ **FIRST TIME SEEING OTHER DAD:** Who knows if this guy can hang? *Ignore him.*

★ **SECOND TIME:** Okay, I see. This guy must live around here and have a kid my age. He's just like me! *Ignore.*

★ **THIRD TIME:** Try out a "What's up?" or a nod. Act like you don't even care. Then: *ignore.*

★ **FOURTH TIME:** Try an icebreaker like, "How old is your kid?" or "Looks like we're both here at the playground again." Stand around awkwardly.

★ **FIFTH TIME:** Try something like, "Look, I don't know if this is crazy or not, but I think you and I could have something special if only we could break down these walls between us. Isn't this silly? To be so close and so similar and have this uncrossable bridge? Let's tear it down and let this thing grow and blossom like I know it can," or "Hey," then *ignore.*

DAD FRIENDS ARE LIKE WAR BUDDIES

Even if he doesn't turn out to be "The One," dad friendships can grow over the years. When you're making sure your toddlers don't hit each other, small talk with other parents might seem unnecessary. But as kids get bigger, you'll graduate to bench-sitting buddies, happily ignoring your kids. Just like guys stuck in a foxhole, you'll have a life-long bond because you've seen some shit together.

OTHER TODDLERS' PARENTS: A FIELD GUIDE

Anyone can spot a helicopter parent, no problem. But what about the other kinds of parents? That's a little harder, but I'll hook you up. Have fun categorizing your family and friends!

★ **EXPLAINERS:** These parents think toddlers can be reasoned with, that if the logic behind a situation is explained effectively, then their kids won't be brats anymore.

   Can be heard saying: "Now Desmond, while it's true it's your ball, how would you feel if another child didn't want to share with you? Being civil to one another is all part of the social contract that protects all of us from falling into anarchy."

★ **SHOUT-THREE-TIMES-THEN-GIVE-UPPERS:** These parents will shout at their kids three times, get no results, and then give up. They understand that they must exert control but are unable to get results, so the *appearance* of caring will have to do.

   Can be heard saying: "Cassidy, get off the fence. Off the fence, Cassidy! Cassidy! Off! The! Fence! Oh, whatever." [Parent sobs while Cassidy climbs the fence.]

- ★ **APOLOGISTS:** These parents' kids aren't out of control, you just don't know their kids like they do. Their kids are not monsters, they're really sweet, somewhere way, way, way deep inside.

  Can be heard saying: "You know, I think Charlotte is upset because Wednesdays are normally our day at the garden, but today we went to music class instead. And she only drank half of her smoothie this morning, and she's dropping a nap and teething and her dad just left on a trip, so . . ."

- ★ **SPACE CADETS:** These parents are asleep at the wheel, except they might have forgotten to bring the wheel. They're out to lunch, except they forgot to bring lunch. You get what I'm saying; they're spaced out.

  Can be heard saying: "I can only think of two poems about clouds and I might have dreamed one of them."

- ★ **AT-THEIR-WITS'-ENDS:** Banana-smeared stroller and dirty-faced kids in tow, giant tote bags with who knows what in them, these parents are one "Get Down!" from a full-blown meltdown.

  Can be heard saying: "I'm sorry I didn't bring your tiara, Madison. Violet, you'll have to share. I don't want to hear it!"

- ★ **DRILL SERGEANTS:** Get in line, Private. These parents will not tolerate wiggles on the subway or any *antics*. Discipline, close talking, and being a tyrant will have you wishing you could adopt these assholes' kids.

  Can be heard saying: "Francis, do you think it is appropriate to be standing there? Sit your ass down."

- ★ **FUNNEST DADS EVER:** These guys are chasing kids around, being "monsters" at the playground. They've got bubble guns shooting awesome bubbles everywhere. The kids at the playground love it! These guys are exhausting.

Can be heard saying: "I'm coming to GET YOUUUUUU!"

★ **BIG MEETING PARENTS:** These parents are multitasking their asses off, taking full advantage of the mobile workplace to ignore their kids.

Can be heard saying: "Look, I'm losing you, but definitely cc me on that and—honey, you have to fill the balloon yourself—let's circle back to this on Thursday."

★ **SHERPAS:** Guiding their children through a spiritual journey, these parents are all about exposing their kids to multicultural offerings that can expand their minds. Sand mandalas, yoga, bitter ethnic food—all of these are parts of the path to enlightenment.

Can be heard saying: "Honey, are you going to finish your doro wat, or are you feeling fully nourished already?"

★ **COACH DADS:** These guys are ex-athletes and huge sportsball fans with an exhaustive knowledge of proper stances and awesome attitudes. Until they start losing.

Can be heard saying: "Good hustle! That's the intensity! What the hell are you doing, Kyle?!?"

★ **WINGIN' ITS:** No plan, no snacks, no phone charger, no money; it's as if these guys are immune to anxiety in a truly disturbing way. The rest of us are picking up the slack around here, man!

Can be heard saying: "Mind if we bum a few raisins from you, man?"

★ **HIPSTER DADS:** Mustaches, hats, tats; these dads haven't let their kids slow them down a bit. If anything, the little ones have opened them up to some pretty cool music.

    Can be heard saying: "Yeah, I'm really getting into Afropop; Dirk just goes crazy for it."

★ **JUST BASICALLY THE BEST DAD EVER:** This dad is incredibly charming and clever, and somehow he manages to be handsome and caring.

    Can be heard saying: "Hi, my name is Doug Moe." (A man can dream, right?)

SAVOR THE MOMENT

When your kid is little, people will tell you: *"Savor the moment."*

    Savor the moment. Savor every precious moment! They grow up so fast. Savor the hugs, savor the kisses, even savor the tears.

    Savor the diapers. Soon they'll be walking, so savor the crawling. Savor the tantrums, savor the screaming!

    Savor the complaining, savor the broken toy bought a week ago. I hope you didn't get ANGRY! Try SAVORING instead.

    Savor. Savor. Savor! Savor every goddamn moment, you ungrateful lout. Were you hoping to put your kid to bed early instead of savoring him? I'm not sure you're getting this savoring thing.

    Savor it all! Savor getting socked in the nuts, savor stepping on sharp Legos, savor no sleep. Slather yourself in savoring, pour that hot soup of savoring in your lap and slosh it around in your pants. Smile, you POS non-savorer! Let the savoring wash over you like you're a pig on a platter being basted in your own savory sauces.

    Savor the moment.

DEVELOPMENTAL MILESTONES: WHAT'S UP WITH MY TODDLER?

What's up with my toddler? Still a lot of interesting developments!

★ **TODDLERS CAN WALK BY THEMSELVES,** but they prefer company.

★ **TODDLERS BEGIN TO RUN,** but you can still totally lap them.

★ **TODDLERS CAN KICK BALLS,** so it's time to review sportsball contract law.

★ **TODDLERS MAKE BELIEVE,** like making believe that they don't have to go to bed ever.

★ **TODDLERS LIKE OTHER CHILDREN,** even that kid Trevor from next door.

★ **TODDLERS IMITATE OTHERS,** but they are sillier and chubbier.

★ **TODDLERS CAN SORT THINGS BY SHAPE AND COLOR,** but they still don't understand recycling rules.

CHAPTER SIX

MAN ★ VS. ★ LITTLE KID

WHO AM I KIDDING? LITTLE KIDS ARE EASY!

YOU'VE GOT A LITTLE KID NOW

Before you know it, a terrible thing has happened: Your toddler is going to preschool, reading, and loves your iPad more than you. He's a full-blown kid now: the first step in becoming an adult and leaving you forever. At least for now, he's just a little kid—a still adorable phase that can be bewildering and maddening in new ways. But the world loves a little kid.

And what's not to like? Little kids are the perfect size to hustle around town. They're full of questions, curiosity, and wonder. Perfect for museums, music classes, and dare I say . . . brunch?

Hmmm . . . museums, music, brunch . . . Starting to sound familiar? You've got your old life back, pal! Sort of.

SHOULD I WORRY IF MY KID TALKS WEIRD?

Nah. I've never liked little kids who speak like they're adults: "Gosh, Mrs. Johnson, dogs sure can be funny animals!" UGH. Stow it, kid. These precocious little busybodies think they're *so damn great* talkin' pretty so quickly. And when I see a kid in a tiny vest and bow tie, I wanna give him a noogie, right quick, to show him who's boss.

No, I like my kids to be kids. And one of the surest signs that your kid is turning into an adult is when they start saying things correctly. What a heartache!

Remember when you had a tiny toddler who would say "Gaygosh," and you and your wife were the only ones who knew that meant

"Gator," the stuffed animal platypus that he thought was an alligator? Adorable.

Or that "baba" meant "bottle," but "bawa" meant "bye-bye," so when he dropped his bottle he'd say, "Bawa baba" and start crying? So sweet.

Or that dogs were "wogs"? And "cabs" were "cats" and "cats" were "cabs," so it sounded like he wanted to call a cat and get a pet cab. So silly!

Now, suddenly, your child is saying things correctly. "Book," "toys," and "I'm angry." It's like he's almost . . . a grown-up.

Nonsense is underrated. It's *cute!* They can stay cute awhile, can't they? I'll take "dada" over "father" any day of the week. Pronunciation, logic, critical thinking: What has any of that ever done for us?

So I say hold onto their youth! Let them talk in a garbled mishmash of pidgin English until they're off living in their own "how-wows" with their pet cabs.

PRESCHOOL: SWEET, SWEET FREEDOM

Maybe you've been cobbling together some combination of nannies, babysitters, Nana, and staying at home, but now you need to go back to work. It's time for (pre)school.

PRESCHOOL IS BETTER THAN YOU WILL EVER BE

It is a hard decision to turn your child over to someone else. But if you're lucky, people with far more patience than you will teach your kid yoga, splatter painting, and sharing. Sure, it'll mean a lot less time with your kid, but let's face it: Preschool is a better version of you:

★ Preschool has art supplies, not just printer paper, half-rinsed-out yogurt containers and a stack of old *New Yorkers*.

★ Preschool has healthy snacks, not "half your muffin."

★ Preschool has attentive teachers, not you on your phone.

Maybe I'm being a little tough on you. You've tried hard, but everybody half-asses it sometimes. I mean, not preschool; they don't.

DROP-OFF: THE LOSE-LOSE

A lot of kids have separation anxiety and freak out when you drop them off. This is perfectly normal. It's best not to compare this to *Sophie's Choice* in any way. The way your child screams and reaches out to you as a stranger tears him from your arms is totally different from Meryl Streep handing her kid to the Nazis. These aren't Nazis; they're way more fun. You want to say: *It's okay; you'll get to do Play-Doh today!* But you also know that you must leave as quickly as possible and trust he'll calm down.

Or maybe you've got one of those kids that barely looks back to say good-bye, sprinting off to join the other kids with nary a "Peace out, Dad" to be had. WTF. Maybe that hurts even more; after all, you're gonna miss the little bugger. Peep in the window and take a look: There he is yukking it up with his pals. Geesh. Way to throw ol' Dad to the curb.

HOW WILL I KNOW IF THE PRESCHOOL IS GOOD?

You'll know how good the preschool is by the number of art projects your child is sent home with. Every month, good preschools send home:

- ★ 1–20 paper-plate projects (clocks, drawings, sundials, etc.)
- ★ 3–15 paintings (large-scale splatter paintings, color-theory exercises, "self-portraits," etc.)
- ★ 4–7 mixed-media paste-and-tissue paper collages
- ★ 2 hand turkeys
- ★ 9 puppets
- ★ 4 clay bowls
- ★ 600–1,347 "drawings"

If no art is coming home, this may not be a sign of a problem; it may be accumulating in a bin that will be emptied all at once. In this case, the art will ruin your home in one fell swoop. DO NOT THROW AWAY ANY ART.

CAN I AFFORD PRESCHOOL?

No, you definitely can't! Maybe you'd be better off not working, but then you'd be depriving your child of creative exploration and social acclimation and dooming him to be forever behind his peers. Maybe just send him to extended days on Tuesdays and Thursdays.

WITH GREAT POWER COMES WEIRD OPINIONS

Now that your kid is talking, what the hell is he talking about? It's amazing how language acquisition works. And as children learn more of the world . . . well let's just say that "kids say the darnedest things."

They have weird ideas because they don't understand how the world works yet. Now that they can express themselves, let's figure out what the hell they're talking about.

"MAYBE INDIA IS IN A MUSEUM!"

Kids don't understand death. When our cat India died, my daughter asked if our family pet was in a museum now. As she explained: Dinosaurs died and then they were put in a museum. So is that where India was?

Kids have no understanding of the concept of death or how you either A) live forever in heaven after you die, or B) this whole thing has been a terrible lie and we are basically a highly functioning stack of chemicals.

"BUT I WANT IT!"

Kids don't understand that wishing something doesn't make it true. They don't know about heartache yet, they've never been in a band that practiced really hard but never put out an album, and they haven't read *The Secret*. Wanting something doesn't make it so—unless you beg and whine hard enough.

"YOU MADE ME TRIP!"

Kids don't understand cause and effect—or blame. They'll hit their heads on playground railings and blame the railings. Or they'll fall over while running to you and blame you. Then again, your parents are to blame for most of your disappointing life choices, so kids might be onto something.

"YES!"

Kids don't understand the word *no*. They love *saying* "no," but they don't much like hearing it.

"WHAT CAN I BUY FOR SIXTY-EIGHT CENTS?"

Nothing. You can't buy anything. Be careful; it seems like a good idea to teach your kids the value of money, except that once they understand, they will realize you are being cheap.

THE IPAD YOU USED TO HAVE

You used to have an iPad. Now, it seems, your child has one. You never see it anymore, and when you do, it's never charged and it's filthy. Another one of your cool gadgets has become a jelly-smeared ruin.

Kids LOVE iPads and smartphones. It's almost sickening to see your child hunched over the device, mindlessly swiping, oblivious to the world around her. *Who does that?*

HIDDEN HORROR OF PARENTING: THE DILLYDALLY

One underappreciated horror of parenting is the constant dillydallying. Much emphasis is placed on dirty diapers, crying, whining, and tantrums, but the slow Chinese water torture of the dillydally is worse.

It turns the most basic activity into a drawn-out exercise in frustration. Getting out the door becomes an epic struggle. Getting ready for bed takes all night. And it should be so easy. Take putting on pajamas, for example. Nothing to it, right? The steps are clear.

1. Take off current clothing.
2. Put on pajamas.

But inside the mind of your dillydallying child, these are the steps:

1. Take off the shirt.
2. Throw the shirt in the air!
3. Try to catch the shirt.
4. I can definitely catch this shirt if only I throw it eighteen times!
5. Uh oh, the shirt is stuck on a high shelf. Yay! A mission for a HERO!
6. Pull the shirt and knock my dragon, Lily, off the shelf. Oh no! Lily! Lily, I am sorry! I'm so sorry, Lily! Are you okay, Lily?! I will give you snuggles, Lily. . . .

7. Markers! There are markers here on the floor where I have left them for several weeks. I will draw something.

8. Is there paper, Dad?

9. Dad just said something. Oh. "Put on your pajamas." That's what I'm DOING!

10. Take pants off. Could I get my underwear off without taking my pants off? Probably!

11. Pants are stuck on my feet.

12. Shuffle dance, shuffle dance. Ice-skate, ice-skate around the house.

13. Ouch! I fell over! How did this happen? Why, why, why?! Ooooh! Whaaa!

14. Pants off.

15. I'm NAKED. Run, run, RUN! Naked run, naked run around the house.

16. Underwear back on. Pajama bottoms on.

17. Pajama top stuck on head. I can't see! I can't see! My arm is stuck. Now I am a zombie. Muuuuuhhhh . . . Zombie walk.

18. I'm stepping on something. . . . Oh no! Lily! I'm sorry, Lily!

19. Pajamas fully on. HOW IS IT BEDTIME? THIS IS SOME BS.

Imagine having that much fun doing something routine. Great for kids, a horror for parents.

The dillydally is the worst.

Before your device becomes another total casualty of becoming a parent, get control. Snap out of it, man!

YOUR KID SHOULDN'T BE ON THE DEVICE IN THE FIRST PLACE

Yes, of course. That is true. Oh well. Whatever momentary lapse of judgment brought you here, here we are. And after all, pretending that the phone only works for grown-ups stopped making sense at a certain point. Dwelling in the past isn't going to help us.

YOU NEVER GET TO USE IT

Maybe she'd let you borrow it? I'm kidding, but really maybe you should learn to share or take turns. Take advantage of your greater understanding of how time works to trick your kid into forfeiting the iDevice for longer periods of time. When it's "her turn," perhaps it is "out of batteries."

SOMETHING HARD HAS CONGEALED ON IT

Is there something in your house that doesn't yet have something congealed on it? Congealing is a major feature of having a kid. It's good practice to occasionally clean your phone, and by extension, other parts of your house. Baby steps, baby steps.

PEOPLE ARE JUDGING YOU

Other people are watching you let your kid play on the device while you are eating out or sitting on the subway. Okay, maybe they are judging you for letting your kid veg out. Or maybe they're judging you for something totally different! You might be fucking up multiple things. The point is, it's hard to please people, so why bother to try? Enjoy your peace however you get it.

THE APP STORE IS RUINING YOUR LIFE

Remember when "shopping" was going to some store only to find out they didn't have what you wanted, so you had to buy some other dumb thing that disappointed you? The App Store brings that disappointment to your living room.

Naturally, you've locked down those purchases with a passcode, but it won't stop the begging and whining for new apps. So make up some new restriction: No apps over 173 MB (try explaning megabytes to a kid), only two apps a month, or delete one app to get another.

WHAT ARE THESE "IN-APP PURCHASES"?

"Sir, the charges are coming from *inside the house*!" My wife once got a call from our credit card company about suspicious charges, only to find our daughter was in the living room buying "fairy treasure" or something via in-app purchases. These are charges that appear in most of the "free" apps.

WHAT IF I NEVER GET MY IPAD BACK?

That's what your phone is for.

HOW TO DO FUN STUFF WHEN YOUR LITTLE KID IS SCARED OF EVERYTHING

Sometimes your little kid won't want to do something fun because it's scary. Really? That little slide is scary? But when you're a kid, lots of things are SCARY.

I remember when I was a kid, we had a few books around that used to freak me out. One was *History of Art*, in which I found medieval Hieronymus Bosch paintings with insane birdmen and people being burned alive in hell. Yeah, SCARY. I mean, Bosch was *trying* to be scary. But lots of other random things freaked me out, too:

★ The robber in Maurice Sendak's *Pierre*. Even though a lion immediately ate him, I was really scared of robbers.

★ The wind in Maurice Sendak's *Chicken Soup with Rice*. It had this freaky face on it.

★ The goat-faced Wild Thing in Maurice Sendak's . . . You know what? I think Maurice Sendak scared the shit out of me.

Anyway, kids are scared of lots of unpredictable things. Like:

★ Your mother
★ A pile of clothes
★ Someone suddenly saying "Hi!"
★ That one perfectly nice babysitter
★ That expensive toy you bought
★ Closets
★ Big dogs
★ That Talking Heads song
★ That statue of Chester Alan Arthur in Madison Square Park

Fear is irrational. People spend time worrying about terrorism when they should be worrying about cholesterol or traffic accidents.

But fear gives us moments where dads can shine. This is what we call a win-win.

USE AN OLD DAD RESPONSE: "GROW A PAIR!"

Sometimes your kid *does* need to grow a pair. It's true. Sometimes facing your fears and/or having your fears ignored and dismissed by the people you love the most is just the thing to get you over your fear. So if you callously tell your kid to "get over it," know that you are in a long line of he-men whose rugged determination and ability to bury fear deep in the pits of their stomachs made this country great.

USE A NEW DAD RESPONSE: "IT'S GONNA BE OKAY."

Tenderness, understanding, and acknowledging feelings: This is the New Dad. Being heard and feeling respected definitely feels nice. I don't always remember to be this way, but when I do, it feels like I have overcome some deep-seated harmful tradition. Dare I say that there is nothing to fear but fear itself?

If one method doesn't work, try the other one. Pretty soon, you'll have a little adrenaline junkie on your hands. And if you never scare your kid, you'll miss out on doing all sorts of things. What are you going to do, never look at statues of Chester Alan Arthur?

HELP, MY KID IS A TINY HOARDER

Purging is a foreign concept for little kids. Why do they love those shitty plastic whistles they get from birthday parties so much? Look at all the junk they are accumulating. Have you seen that show about hoarders? You know, *Hoarders*? That's your kid.

On *Hoarders*, the crew enters a seemingly normal home to find that there are rooms full of giant stacks of newspapers, and where there are no newspapers, there are dead cats. In the refrigerator, which hasn't worked for years, there are jars of mayonnaise so old that mayonnaise is called "Dr. Bronson's Miracle Mayonnaise Cure."

Luckily, an expert has been brought in to assess the situation. This kind and understanding person patiently looks through the hoarders' "collections" and assures the hoarders that nothing— *nothing*—will be thrown away without their permission.

Next, a crew starts to throw away the piles of garbage. Garbage that was actually part of the hoarder's precious "collections." Trust is lost; nothing can be thrown away. Now the hoarder is sobbing and having a tantrum.

Sound familiar?

HIDDEN HORROR OF PARENTING:
A THOUSAND TINY CUTS

There are many more minor annoyances that cumulatively drive you mad. Parenting is like a thousand tiny cuts

1. Leaning on you all the time: Stand up, dude!
2. Climbing on top of you with no warning.
3. Pulling on your arm and almost knocking you over.
4. Making you carry a million little things, each of which, if lost, will be a tragedy of epic proportions.
5. Making hot food for them that is forgotten and gets cold and then they want new food.
6. Dropping ice cream on the ground: Now they want a new one.
7. Not letting you throw out any of their broken garbage.
8. Fishing things out of the garbage that you DID throw out: They find and resurrect junk like a horror movie.
9. Having to buy something for them whenever you go anywhere.
10. Making you get quarters so they can ride those mechanical horses in front of grocery stores.
11. Skipping naps and then getting cranky and then falling asleep on the way home and ruining bedtime, too.

12. Hitting other kids right in front of you so you have to address it.

13. Stealing toys, but in really obvious ways: No finesse.

14. Going around and around you forever.

15. Going up and down hallways forever.

16. Going up and down the stairs forever.

17. Wanting to be carried.

18. Wanting to be put down.

19. Wanting to be picked up again.

20. Getting their fingers pinched in doors.

21. Getting their fingers pinched in cabinets.

22. Getting their fingers pinched in strollers.

23. Getting their fingers pinched in high chairs.

24. Being "bored."

25. Feeling "car sick."

26. Wanting to know "how much longer until we get there."

27. Feeling cold and wanting the air conditioner turned down.

28. Feeling too hot now.

29. Wanting to know if "we're there yet."

30. Wanting to sleep in your bed.

31. Getting a big kid bed and then not wanting to sleep in it.

32. Not being tired: How is that possible?

Oh man. I gotta take a walk; I'm getting worked up just writing this list.

BACK IN THE GOOD OLD DAYS

In the olden days, a child would get a single precious toy, such as a handmade doll named Baby Doll, and it would be treasured until the day the crick done come and took it. Then Pa would carve up a small mossy log, making a slightly sadder Baby Doll 2.

Ah, the good old days. A single, sad baby doll would be the perfect amount of toys for your one-and-a-half bedroom apartment.

ANYTHING CAN BE A "COLLECTION"

Nowadays, kids acquire objects all the time. Any group of objects can become a "collection." These items can include:

★ Birthday party goody bags full of cheap junk

★ Business cards, plastic stirring straws, and napkins from the deli

★ "Art" projects and other creations made during misguided "creative time"

★ Presents that must never be discarded, even when they are never used

★ Delivery boxes for things that you ordered that were actually useful and definitely not junk

YOU WILL HAVE THIS JUNK FOREVER

You still have that box of junk at your parent's place that they keep bugging you about, right? It's crazy that they care, since they have PLENTY OF ROOM, but these are the stakes. Just like you will never get that box, your child will never get rid of his stuff and you'll be stuck with it forever. That's what we're talking about here: boxes of junk that will remain in your house for all of eternity.

HOW TO THROW THINGS AWAY

The main lesson from *Hoarders* is that if you want to throw things away, it is best to do it secretly, behind the hoarders' backs. The same lesson applies to your tiny hoarder.

★ **DO NOT RECYCLE:** I can't count the number of "art projects" my daughter has retrieved from the paper recycling because my eco-guilt trumped common sense. Just put this in the trash, straightaway. You'll have to save the environment later.

★ **PURGATORY ISN'T JUST FOR CATHOLIC SINNERS:** If you haven't the heart for full secretive purging, find a spot to squirrel away collections for a bit: a purgatory for toys and junk. If your child notices their absence in a set period of time, they can be "resurrected," otherwise they may be damned to the junk heap.

★ **"DONATIONS FOR BABIES":** Some kids may be convinced to donate old toys to unspecified "babies" that need them. Maybe there are even actual babies you know. My daughter never gave a shit about these "babies," but maybe you are a better liar than me.

And just like on *Hoarders*, intervention has a spotty track record with this problem. If you're lucky, your tiny hoarder will learn the value of minimalism, of only keeping those objects that spark joy in her heart. But most tiny hoarders continue to suffer from this affliction until they leave the house and you put their stuff on the curb to make their bedrooms into a crafting rooms. Good luck.

HELP, MY KID LOOKS LIKE A TINY HOBO

Your kid has a favorite costume he won't take off. It's acquiring a certain smell and level of filth that you're not comfortable with. You have a tiny hobo.

THE MAD PRINCESS

Our daughter went through a serious princess phase during which she refused to take off her purple dress and purple princess hat. Needless to say, these were unwashable, all delicate lace and special fabrics. Over time, the dress acquired a certain hobo-osity. It had brown stains and permanent food on it; the lacy parts had rips and tears; and it didn't clasp in the back anymore. Much more Broom-Hilda than Cinderella. Hobo-osity. The charm had worn off big time.

The problem was that she didn't care. The little kid heart wants what it wants. She'd look in the mirror and see no filth, no stains. She was like an old crone that looks into her magic mirror and only sees a young beauty staring back.

Meanwhile, all the other parents at IKEA stared at her, judging me. But they were buying birch-colored Blürgs, so what do they know?

SUPER-DIRTY MAN

Boys aren't any better. It's commonplace to see little boys in their disgusting Superman costumes around town, off–Halloween season, with parents that don't care or don't want to fight. Wouldn't the Justice League be like, "Superman, buddy, you *gotta* wash yourself. Is Tide your Kryptonite? At least wash that red underwear. Hey, Wonder Twins, how about 'Form of a Washing Machine?' Gleek can do some scrubbing."

DOES IT MATTER IF EVERY DAY IS HALLOWEEN?

Then again, who cares? When you have kids, you gotta let them dress crazy. Nothing's sadder to me than a kid in a business suit. Let your kid be crazy! He'll be a corporate lawyer for the rest of his life, so let him be a Spiderman for a few years.

But if you can't shake the concern that it reflects poorly on you, here are a few ideas to clean up your Mini-Mess.

BATMAN VS. THE HULK

Who would win in a fight: Batman or the Hulk? I know, I know, they don't live in the same universe, you don't have to tell me, friend. But your kid doesn't know that. Play off his natural desire to be the strongest by talking smack about the Hulk long enough to get the costume in the wash. "Batman is definitely the *best*. Way better than the *Schmulk*."

Once Hulk is clean, it's time to talk trash about the Dark Knight.

BE FAIR TO EVERY PRINCESS

Disney keeps adding new princesses every fiscal year, so take advantage of that to get the full rainbow of princess dresses. When the

Cinderella blues get a little funky, get your daughter to try on the Sleeping Beauty pinks for a while.

GENERIC-MAN TO THE RESCUE!

Branded superheroes are just the Little Kid Industrial Complex's vision of heroism. Make your kid a weird costume from disparate, ever-changing, *washable* parts: a mask, a cape, some boots, and ta-da, you've got a kickass indie hero. When I was a kid, my mom made me a Superman cape, wrong colors and everything, and a Superman mask (*Um, Mom: Superman doesn't wear a mask!*) that I'd supplement by putting a plastic basketball hoop on my head for a crown. And look, I turned out great! Now I'm a comedian!

PLAYING DRESS-UP WITH DIGNITY

Remember playing dress-up with your dad?

You don't? Oh, that's because dads used to have DIGNITY. They were hidden behind newspapers and pipe smoke, too inaccessible to be roped into playing princesses or cops and firemen. Dignity: That's what being a grown-up used to be about. Not to be confused with standoffishness, lack of emotional connection, or needless pride.

Things are different now: You have a pink boa around your neck, a crown on your head, and purple lipstick on your lips. You are a pretty, pretty princess. You're a New Dad, not afraid to mix it up, let loose, and have a little fun. Great. So dignity is not in the cards, but how do you make it through dress-up without feeling like a big idiot?

MAKE IT FUN FOR YOU: SUBVERTING THE NARRATIVE

Your daughter has ingested enough princess stories to know that princes save princesses. What kind of message is that? You want to raise a strong girl. But making princesses save the prince? A little too on the nose. That's why I like to play the creepy dungeon dweller who turns out to be a sweetheart. Or a second princess who got lost on the way to her castle. Make the story weird! *"Excuse me, other princess, I'm looking for the castle with the cupcake shop in the catacombs!"*

And what better time to teach your son about city government? Maybe your fireman is ineffective because he's worried about his pension payments. Or maybe you're a cop on the take. *"It'll cost you eight hundred clams to get me to arrest that ineffective fireman. Yeah, yeah, we're all worried about the social safety net."*

GO NATIVE: FULLY EMBRACING THE MOMENT

Being a parent sometimes just means doing what your kid wants. In improv, we call this "Yes-Anding." You go further by building on your partner's ideas. He wants a fireman to hang out with his policeman? Sure, go for it. Put on your best Boston accent, go gung ho, and start barking out fireman orders. *"Theahs a fiah in the Hahvahd Coop. It's spreading down Comm Ave to Kenmoah Squayah!"*

GET TRAPPED IN A TOWER OR SOMEWHERE ELSE

Tired? Not in the mood to be an active participant today? Any dress-up situation can be subverted to include a trapped (lazy) parent. Princes got locked in towers, train engineers get locked in control rooms, monsters need to sit on couches for a bit. Be hard to rescue—so hard that you get to chill out for a while. *"Troll need a little time on Twitter."*

FULFILL A CHILDHOOD DREAM

Did you always want to be beautiful or graceful or talented? Maybe you always wanted to be a dancer—now's your chance! Your kid has very little critical judgment and is easily impressed by commitment. Belt out your song, dance with abandon, throw off the shackles and play, you wonderful fool! Your kid will never be as blinded by love for you as he is now. *"What an honor to win the first Oscar for Most Incredible Dancing in the Olympics!"*

OOPS, YOU'RE A BIG FAT LIAR NOW

Of course you would never lie to your kid! Me neither. It's just . . . sometimes you need to stretch the truth to get good behavior without too much hassle. To call these "lies" is a bit harsh, although they are lies. Let's call them "alternative facts." These tiny fibs just help grease the wheels a bit. But be careful not to use them too much.

"I'M LEAVING!"

Your kid doesn't want to leave the park, the dance class, the store, so you say, "Okay, I'm leaving! Bye! I guess you're going to stay here tonight." But that never happens. It might work the first few times, scaring your kid into submission, but this becomes a favorite threat of some parents and loses its efficacy quickly.

Your kid knows it's baloney.

- ★ **PARENT:** "I'm leaving!"
- ★ **CHILD:** "Okay, cool. See you later!"
- ★ **PARENT:** "I'm leaving!"
- ★ **CHILD:** "Yeah, you said that. I guess I'll stay here with all these strangers, then!"
- ★ **PARENT:** "I mean it. I guess we'll see you later."
- ★ **CHILD:** "Yep. I GOT IT. I'm sure you mean it, because otherwise that would mean you're a huge liar. BUH-bye!"
- ★ [Parent stays, shamed.]

Use sparingly!

"FIVE MORE MINUTES."

What is time? I know, I know. I can be pretty deep. But isn't time just a way of relating to experience? Five minutes can FEEL different depending on what you're doing. Five minutes of being punched in the face is different than five minutes of eating ice cream. So I use this flexibility to my advantage, especially before kids have mastered the clock.

- ★ "Five more minutes" = Two minutes before we leave the boring library
- ★ "Five more minutes" = Thirty minutes chatting with other parents.
- ★ "Five more minutes" = Five minutes, but followed by another five. Let's call it ten minutes.

While you are the master of time, use this knowledge for good.

"I DON'T HAVE ANY MONEY."

Children don't know how money is made; they're terrible investors, and yet they want to spend and spend. Until they can figure out that you always have your wallet, you can claim you don't have money. When I say this, I mean "I don't have any money for *you*."

★ I don't have *snack money*.
★ I don't have *toy money*.
★ I don't have *donate to endangered pandas money*.

And once they gain wallet awareness, they're probably "earning" an allowance. Let them spend *their* money.

LYING IS TOTALLY FINE AND DOES NO LASTING DAMAGE

Or at least that is what one Internet article told me before I stopped reading it. Anyway, so many things do lasting damage; what are the chances that lying about being "out of cake" is a major problem?

TELLING THE TRUTH ALL THE TIME IS IMPOSSIBLE

Actually, it isn't. Actually, *now* I'm lying. SEE HOW HARD IT IS? So don't split hairs about which lies are okay. That's throwing the baby out with the bathwater, if there ever was bathwater, you big fat liar.

KIDS WANT TO HELP, BUT THEY ARE BAD AT IT

Kids love to "help." They "wanna." This is great but maddening, because tiny tots are *not good at things*. It would be easier to do it yourself, but you know that good parents are out there joyfully baking gluten-free vegan cupcakes with their kids like they are running a bakery or something. Or maybe you want to clean the garage or rake or do some other bit of hard work. And at this very moment, great dads are probably instilling the value of hard work in their kids by happily raking together like it's some kind of Amish rake party.

Yes, kids are adorable. Yes, they are fun to watch trying. But if you want something done, woo, boy, a kid is not who you call.

Okay, *process* is important. But more important than finishing? Clearly, you understand that by getting helped, you are doing more than a job. You are bonding and showing your child how to make his way in the world. It's important for sure. And maybe there's a way to have your cake and have it not be a disgusting, child-ruined cake unworthy of eating, too.

GIVE THEM USELESS JOBS

Sweeping the garage? Someone's got to organize the recycling. Maybe it needs to be color coded. Raking? Kids are perfect for picking up sticks and piling them up somewhere. Point is, there's usually some kind of useless side job that won't interfere with the main one. Isn't *looking* busy a valuable skill to have?

GIVE THEM SPECIAL JOBS

Or maybe your kid can have the "special job" of mixing the flour and sugar. Or stirring. Or something else that is "special" but doesn't happen very often, like moving water from bowl to bowl.

BE DONE

If your kid is truly bad at helping, maybe you are "done." Yes, the living room is half-vacuumed, but maybe that is "done" until he loses interest and bothers his mom. Then you can vacuum the other half.

HEAVY TOOLS ARE HARD TO USE

As dads know, tools are the best part of work. So your kid probably desperately wants to use the rake and won't be satisfied by some pretend rake. So give him the heaviest, most awkward tool you have. This will knock the motivation to work hard right out of him.

DON'T KILL THE GOLDEN GOOSE

If your kid is determined to help you, and you're finding it tough to take, just bear in mind that this is all part of a long-term plan. First: "helping." Then: chores. Soon: part-time job, full-time job, supporting you through your old senile years. It all starts with your daughter failing to use a dustpan properly. Don't kill this golden goose!

LYING IS OKAY IF IT'S PART OF A LONG-STANDING TRADITION

In the olden days, parents told their children that a troll lived under a bridge so they wouldn't wander out of the village and into the woods and be mauled by a bear. Or they said that God would damn them to hell for eternity just to get them to churn some butter. So we've come a long way.

Still, some lies, like Santa or the Easter Bunny, are part of a proud, long-standing tradition of benevolent lies that are totally okay.

LYING IS FUN AND NOBLE

Unlike saying "Grandma is always in our hearts," lying about Santa is fun and noble. Little kids love magic. They see the magic in the mundane. "Look, a pretty boat!" they say, pointing at some half-assed fading mural on the side of a pizzeria, and we love them for it.

Do you want your child to believe only in realism, forgo magic in all its forms, decide that mystery is nothing? That's what you're doing if you don't embrace Santa. Santa is, well, a jolly old elf, and he brings presents. And the anticipation of presents is basically the best thing when you are a kid.

Keep your kid's heart wide open. Don't kill the magic.

KEEP SANTA AND THE REST OF THE MAGICAL CREATURES BELIEVABLE

That said, I like my magical lies to be worthy and credible.

Santa's right on the edge of making no sense. People got too carried away with Santa, added too many insane details for him to sound believable:

★ "Yeah, he lives at the North Pole." *Explains why I never see him, okay.*

★ "And he has a magic sleigh pulled by flying reindeer." *Hmmm, okay reindeer makes sense. . . . And I guess you'd have to fly to get everywhere so quickly.*

★ "And he, uh, comes down your chimney with toys his elves made for you. *Sigh, okay, now you're blowing it for me.*

That's why I think the Elf on the Shelf is a terrible development for Christmas. If you're lying because of *magic* and *gift giving*, then you're telling a good lie. But if you are lying to enforce good behavior because your surveillance elf is watching, we are back in bridge-troll territory.

These snitches are just another bit of Christmas cruft that makes lying seem so much less wholesome. By putting them front and center, it undermines the magic of the whole thing. It's like if, during his State of the Union address, the president said, "Thank God for the drones out there blowing up bad guys." It's like, *Let's not talk about it.*

And at least the Tooth Fairy has a narrow, believable mandate, a mission statement—"Get the teeth, replace with money"—that doesn't beg too many questions. Your useless old teeth go away, and you get money in return. That's it. It's an easy lie to swallow. There's no reason to look this gift horse in the mouth.

But the Easter Bunny is tough. I didn't think there was any reason to pretend that the Easter Bunny was real, but my wife fucked up and did it already. I didn't want my daughter to think too hard about it, lest our mythological house of cards come tumbling down. The Easter Bunny makes no sense. *Why* is he delivering eggs? I ask you, dear wife, why does the Easter Bunny leave a basket of candy out for our child? What's his *motivation*? Hm? If a rabbit had magical powers, wouldn't he just use his powers to grow himself a ton of carrots?

IS IT TIME TO KILL SANTA?

Do you remember when you realized when there was no Santa, no Easter Bunny, no Tooth Fairy? Do you remember when you realized that magic was a trick, that God was dead, that everyone was just a pile of flesh and blood and you had no one but yourself to blame for being miserable?

Not there yet? Did I go too far?

But at some point, you will come to a fork in the road: Is Santa dead? They understand so many things, is it time to ruin Christmas?

NO: GET BETTER AT LYING

If you're lucky, you can extend the Santa lie a little longer by doubling down on your lie and delaying your kid's development. The older she is, the more you need a great cover story to push off the inevitable. A conspiracy theory, a story too good to question, or at least something plausible. Maybe combine the truth ("I'm Santa!") with another lie ("But don't tell Mom. . . . She has no idea.") to get another year of kid belief out of her. ("And I'm on a secret mission . . . to save the world." Maybe?)

THE LONG CON

Then again, my kid has surprised me a few times. At the time of this writing, she is ten years old and had two more years of Santa belief than I expected, as well as several Tooth Fairy payments and a recent delivery of Easter candy from the Easter Bunny. At least she put up a good front: She seemed to be worried that our new cat would scare the Easter Bunny away.

It could be that my wife and I are victims of a long con to get presents, candy, and money. *She* knows that *we* know that we don't *want to know* that she *knows* that as long as Santa exists, presents still exist. And that means we still have a kid, a big kid, yes, but a kid. Not a cynical, magic-debunking tween. Maybe she's not ready to grow up either. It's a nice thought.

AM I DOOMED TO BE A *MAD* DAD?

So many things have fallen out of fashion since the old days: hats with horns, setting burial boats on fire, and having a temper, to name a few. There was a time when having a terrible temper earned you a cool nickname like "Eric the Red-Eyed." And people would say, "You know what? Let him have that castle. I can't deal with that guy."

Now, being mad is frowned upon, and not getting mad is as hard as ever. Maybe it's genetics, maybe it's the *insane* amount of testosterone I have coursing through my *incredibly* virile body, but I get angry and yell too easily, just like my dad.

My dad is a great guy, but he used to fly off the handle when my brother and I were horsing around too much. He'd burst into the den where we were swan diving off the sofa and yell, "This is not a gymnasium!" I think a lot of Old Dads were like this. It's not like they beat us; it's just that they let things build up and annoy them for too long and then they erupted.

So I inherited his temper along with his corny jokes. And yet, I want to do better. Is there a way to be a less mad dad?

REMEMBER TO BREATHE

Tried and true: breathing. Make sure you're breathing. Step back, get a little distance from the insanity. That's the first thing anyone's going to tell you. Breathe. And sometimes when I hear that, I think, *OF COURSE I'M BREATHING!!!!* Which basically means I'm not breathing deeply enough. Calm, deep breaths.

THEY'RE NOT GIVING YOU A HARD TIME; THEY'RE HAVING A HARD TIME

This little nugget of wisdom is one that I wish I'd known earlier. "They're not giving you a hard time; they're having a hard time." In other words, your kid isn't trying to be a jerk, he is just having a shitty time of it. It's so easy to ascribe evil motivation to annoying behavior, but the likelihood is that your kid is not a "bad seed." More likely they need a snack.

LAUGH LIKE YOU ARE A MANIAC

Sometimes, when I'm at my wits' end, I use my inherent comedic sensibilities to transform rage into laughter. I think, *"Why me? What'd I ever do to deserve this?! Oh my God!* And I wallow in my pity in such an exaggerated way that it'll make me laugh. It probably looks crazy, but it works.

JOIN IN THE MADNESS

Is your kid doing something maddening like banging on the cabinet over and over? Try it! Maybe you're being too rigid. A little noisy craziness can be a wonderful release. Try banging the cabinet with him. Maybe now isn't the time to finish work. Letting go and joining in the madness can sometimes get you back on track.

GET UP AND SHUT UP

Sometimes the thing that makes me stop being so angry is to just *stop talking.* If you don't talk, you can't yell. And sometimes, I realize that

I'm just talking up my anger, making me boil over. I stop talking, get up, and remove myself for a few minutes. It's okay to take a break.

You're never going to be able to stop yelling completely. Kids are frustrating! But you can work at it. You can *try*.

IT HAPPENED TO ME: THE ZEN OF STRAWBERRY SHORTCAKE

My daughter watches the worst, most annoying TV shows. They are terrible. But, as I often remind myself, they are not FOR ME.

When I was Un-Childed, I remember having a strong opinion about parents taking responsibility for what their kids watched on TV. I'd always think: *Where are the parents? Why aren't parents monitoring what these kids are watching?*

But now, I understand how hard that is. I understand that you can be a parent, *in a room with your kid*, watching TV, and still have no idea what she is watching. And that is because your self-defense mechanisms have kicked in to protect what little brain you have left.

And when you do force yourself to tune in, it's horrible.

But sometimes, there is beauty to be found in the ugly. Sometimes, the only peace to be found is in wartime. Or as Auguste Rodin once said, "To the artist there is never anything ugly in nature." Okay, I googled that, but you get my point. *Happiness is an inside job.*

And recently, I found that happiness while watching *Strawberry Shortcake*. The "Shortcakes" were doing something at some stupid pie-making contest, and I don't know why, but suddenly, I was enjoying myself. Instead of feeling angry, a wave of relaxation came over me. It was so brainless, so totally stupid, that my mind settled into a peace I hadn't felt all day. The saccharine sweetness of the whole dumb Strawberry Shortcake gang and their dumb hats had me smiling and nodding. *Yes! Raspberry Tart has a point! They SHOULD be sharing ingredients. Oh, Blueberry Muffin, you are a CHARACTER!*

In a way, *Strawberry Shortcake* is like a kid's version of The Real Housewives. It's fabricated and brainless, but the reassuring rhythms of the show have a soothing effect. Watching the housewives fight and bicker should raise your blood pressure, but instead, it does the opposite. It makes you feel GOOD. Sometimes, you need the white noise, you need the confusion, you need the acrimony and the low-stakes pie-making contest or hair-pulling catfight to refocus on your inner peace.

Namaste, Shortcakes.

HIDDEN HORROR OF PARENTING: TERRIBLE GIFTS FROM MISGUIDED PEOPLE

Wonderful, misguided people will give your child terrible gifts without gift receipts. Sure, your kid will love most of these, but isn't that the biggest problem? Why are these people trying to drive a wedge between you and your child?

TALKING TOYS

Like kids, talking toys don't know when to be quiet. It'd be one thing if these toys talked in a normal voice, but they all use the cloying tone of a robot kindergarten teacher. Or Elmo.

When our daughter was little, she had a plastic chair that sang when a child sat down on it, which was always. She also had a horrible plastic triangle that sang the same song over and over, restarting each time you pressed the button: "It's a small . . . It's a small . . . It's a small . . . It's a small . . ."

Which brings us to my current nightmare: the Furby. This thing activates if you accidentally brush it, and *it has no off switch.* "No off switch" should be a violation of the Geneva Conventions. And what does it do when you activate it? It spews nonsense *very enthusiastically.*

FURBY: "OHHH, JubeeeGAH! She-Bop! Hee hee! En-bildegan-a-joo-JU!"
ME: "Furby, SHUT UP!"
FURBY: "UTSHAY, GeebeeBAH! Goo-gen-beep-shah-BOOoom!"

The only hope with talking toys is for the batteries to die, so that you may live. But us dads pride ourselves on having a large reserve of batteries so that we don't run out when the End Times come. So even though it goes against every fiber in our being, a dead battery should never be replaced immediately. Remember that batteries = power. You have the batteries, so you have the power. With luck, your kid will forget that the toy ever sang/spoke/chattered.

GIANT, NON-CITY TOYS

A lack of understanding about Brooklyn apartment sizes has led to us having a creepy, child-size Barbie and two giant teddy bears. I guess, in the middle of the country, a playroom isn't complete without a giant teddy bear stinking up the corner, but in Brooklyn, we like our bears small and artisanal.

Our daughter also has a wonderful wooden castle. It's well built. It's beautiful. It doesn't fold. I'd take a crappy plastic castle that folds over a wonderful wooden castle any day of the week. Your bike folds, the stroller folds, everything must fold.

Toys that don't fold are furniture. You wouldn't buy a child a couch, would you?

THE FIRST COLLECTIBLE

Maybe your child will enjoy the American Girl® series? You know, the one with eighty-one different dolls and accessories and the clothing line that matches dolls to girls so your kid looks like she is toting around her Mini-Me? Sounds like a huge money pit, but distant relatives are happy to provide the first of the eighty-one installments in this collectible series and let you get the rest.

Nothing sparks a child's interest more than the knowledge that she can acquire four hundred more toys if only they keep the series going. I'm not sure there even is a stand-alone toy anymore. Collectibles are a horror.

CREATIVE GIFTS THAT NEED YOUR HELP

Everyone wants a creative kid. But at what cost? Your time, that's what. From tiny, beginner crochet projects to model cars, your child will need your help. These projects are so full of promise, so exciting to *start*. But do they ever end?

Most of them have steep learning curves and frustrating directions. You will have to help your kid, if possible, all while keeping your own shit together. If the impossible Pom-Pom Puppies project goes awry, will this kill your child's nascent creativity? Will he end up a frustrated artist? If Hitler's aunt hadn't gotten him that friendship-bracelet kit with confusing directions, might history have been different?

GLITTER

Glitter is a scourge. No parent in his right mind would allow a gift of glitter to enter his home. But what if it is disguised as "glitter glue" or glitter kits? What then? Glitter finds a way.

Truthfully, there's not much to do. Glitter will be part of your life, and if you're like me, it will nest in the crook of your nose or high on your forehead and never leave, no matter how much you rub. Glitter is like an untreatable STD: It never goes away. Everyone will know just by looking at you that have a child at home. And like an STD, it's extremely communicable.

TOYS WITH TINY PIECES THAT MUST NOT BE LOST

Our daughter had these little Disney Princess toys that had microscopic slippers the size of half a Valium. God forbid one of Cinderella's matching blue slippers fell under the couch. I'd be combing through dust bunnies for days to find that tiny slipper. Tiny parts designed by childless madmen are to be avoided at all costs. Eventually, if you get good enough at losing accessories, your naked princess toys will be enjoyed in peace. But until then, you will be stuck in the folly of maintaining this tiny inventory of slippers, crowns, and swords.

Gifts are a horror!

COOL BEARDED DADS

Whenever I see a really cool dad with a carefully handcrafted beard, I feel a pang of regret in my stomach. *Could I be a cool dad, too, if only I tried harder?* We all try a little bit to be a cool dad, but some of these dads out there are making the rest of us look bad by being *way* too cool. Also, they won't hang out with me, no matter how many times I ask.

OLD COOL DAD, NEW COOL DAD

It used to be that a "cool dad" was the guy who threw you in the pool or had a little too much to drink and let you burn things. Now, a cool dad is indistinguishable from a cool non-dad. I'm not going to complain about hipsters, but I can't cotton to dads that show no sign of dadness, as if they're still baristas, just with babies. *Baristas with Babies*: Who wants to watch that show?

COOL BEARDED DADS

I knew my rent was going up when I saw a dad with a Salvador Dalí–style mustache move into my neighborhood. I've been lucky enough to live in the slightly less-fashionable area of Brooklyn for long enough that this decorative facial hair is still relatively rare. In Williamsburg, the streets are lousy with mustachioed fathers and tatted-up punk-rock mamas. This level of cool has always eluded me. I think having a kid knocks you down at least two levels of cool, so think of how cool some of these dads were when they weren't even dads. VERY COOL.

CHILDREN WILL FIX THIS

But children are the great levelers. I take some small consolation in picturing the upchuck accident that ruins some hipster dad's cool orange sweater that I could never pull off. I happily contemplate a kid screeching at his dad, "Alex Chilton is a stinky poo-poo, and I don't wanna listen to him anymore!" before smashing his vinyl.

If your dad is this cool, what are you supposed to rebel against? Maybe the final consolation is that by being so solidly lame, I've provided my child with a perfect foil. I've ensured that she will grow

DO YOUR FRIENDS KNOW YOU HAVE A CHILD?

Sometimes, your friends stop paying attention and clearly aren't sure if you have a child. Here's how to find out:

★ **"HOW'S THE FAMILY?"** This is code for not remembering how many kids you have, if any.

★ **"HOW'S THE BABY?"** This person has no idea that you have a ten-year-old. He has let ten years pass without considering that this kid has been growing.

★ **"HOW'S THE KID? SHE'S IN . . . FOURTH GRADE?"** UM, OKAY, buddy. Calm down. Don't worry so much about my kid, okay?

and discover cool things on her own. And isn't that what parenting is about?

(Cool bearded dads: Call me.)

YELLING AT OTHER KIDS ON THE PLAYGROUND

Sometimes, you must tell other people's kids to fuck off.

I think this is fine, but this is not a universally held opinion. In our litigious, helicopter-parent, poverty-of-the-commons world, some people choose to turn a blind eye to other children's misdeeds. But where does this refusal to intervene in civic life end?

Whatever happened to "It takes a village"? Does it only take a village if the village is full of great kids? Shouldn't someone say "This village is fucked?"

BUT DON'T LAY A HAND ON THAT OTHER KID

Touching is a no-no. Parents will not be sympathetic to you grabbing their kids. Hands off! Unless those other kids are pummeling someone.

Again, I'm not talking about intervening in some crime in progress. I'm talking about telling some cretin who's blocking the slide from all the little kids to *make with the sliding*. Or telling some miscreant that it's not okay to write *fart* over and over near your child's chalk rainbow. Most kids spook pretty easily when a strange man comes over and talks to them. I don't try to be extra menacing or anything. But some of these mini serial killers haven't ever had someone tell them no or set their foot down. The way I figure it, I am doing them a big favor. The NOs start here.

WHAT IF ANOTHER PARENT IS MAD AT ME?

If you refuse to talk to another child because you are worried that another parent will get mad at you, then you are telling me that the parent is the boss of you, and by extension, his child is the boss of you. Some strange asshole kid is the boss of you!

If another parent is going to yell at you in front of a bunch of kids, he doesn't deserve your respect. Who cares? A little guidance from a fair-minded, and may I say handsome, man such as yourself should be welcome.

But sometimes you'll encounter a particularly defiant kid, a demon child who does not give a shit. In this case, I'd be especially careful. It may be better to live your life and move along to another part of the playground. These demon kids have demon dads, and you don't need that kind of trouble. Namaste.

SO YOUR KID CAN'T HANDLE A REAL MUSEUM

Children's museums are like children's music: not good but maybe all your spastic, distracted child can handle. Like a lot of "education," it's more about having a good experience than being able to fully comprehend a concept.

GOOD FEELINGS ABOUT ELECTRICITY

Don't worry about whether your kid understands why cranking a handle around and around makes a lightbulb turn on. If the designers of the exhibit couldn't make it clear, your half-assed explanations about it won't help. Don't bore your child. The point is to have a good feeling about learning, not necessarily to learn. Also, I still don't understand electricity except to fear it.

PLAYGROUND OR MUSEUM? WHO CAN SAY?

Some parts of a children's museum seem a lot like a playground. Be happy about that. That's fine. Who knows, maybe going down a slide shaped like an airplane will teach your kid something. He wants to be at the playground anyway. And if you're here instead, it's probably really cold out.

THE POST-RIOT TRASHED BODEGA EXHIBIT

In Brooklyn, we have a children's museum, which shall remain nameless, except to say that it is in *Brooklyn* and is a *Children's Museum*. It has many wonderful exhibits. One of the not-so-great ones is the *Post-Riot Trashed Bodega*. Or I assume that's what it is. I think originally it was a "store" where kids could pretend to sell things, but a mob of horrible children must have passed through and trashed the place. This is a frequent problem of children's museums: all the fucking children.

PREP FOR REAL MUSEUMS

After a few visits to the children's museum, you might be bored with learning how water flows or what an ant farm looks like. You might be yearning for real art. If you've played your cards right, all this time in a "museum" will pay off with an interest in museums in general. Pretty soon, your kid will be wowing kids at his preschool with his theories on decontextualization and representation in art. Good work! Now it's time to ruin a real museum.

HOW TO EXPOSE YOUR KID TO ART WITHOUT FREAKING THEM OUT

I live in New York City, home to some of the greatest art museums in the world. So naturally, I've been relentless in my quest to expose my child to art, even when she was uninterested. Exposing your child to art is one of the greatest gifts you can bestow on them, especially if you aren't incredibly attractive or athletic. Then you're relying on developing their "creativity" to keep them from becoming a deadbeat.

But are art museums all upsides? Sadly, no. There are a few things to bear in mind.

ART IS FULL OF PENISES

I'm not against penises, but I bet you don't notice how many penises there are in artwork until you have a child in tow. And a lot of these phalluses take you by surprise, popping up unexpectedly like they do.

In fact, it's a reoccurring problem of art that the naughty bits appear without warning. It's easy enough to avoid an exhibit that's called *Lots of Penises*, but curators rarely title their exhibits so help-fully. It's more likely that you'll be looking at an exhibit called *Trains!*, and there'll be some sick model train with a penis on it, and then your kid will have disturbing questions about how Thomas reproduces.

ANCIENT GREEK ART: NSFW

Mostly, ancient Greek art is fine; their scantily clad sculptures aren't terribly embarrassing. After all, the human body is nothing to be ashamed of. Just don't look at the vases too closely—the Greeks were innovators in porno vases. Subsequent ancient cultures invented paper and, eventually, the Internet, which made porn much more hideable. In ancient Greece, only the biggest pervs had giant vase collections.

ALL VIDEO INSTALLATIONS ARE SCARY

For some reason, all video art is disturbing. If you make uplifting vid-eos, you put them on YouTube and hope to go viral. If you make sad, repetitive, disturbing videos about dolls getting their hair shorn off, you make "video art." Video art is almost always "too scary." Usually, there will be moaning from the other room and darkness. Peeking around the corner, your kid will first be excited about "watching TV." Then your kid will "want to go home."

SAD LOOKING TOYS ALL KNIT TOGETHER IN A PILE

Another commonly "scary" art exhibit is the pile of sad-looking stained stuffed animals, maybe sewn together to express something horrible about childhood. Or maybe it's a bunch of Barbie dolls half-buried in sand. Or a rickety baby carriage with a stuffed crow in it. You know, something that reminds you of that weird daycare down the street. Children can't yet appreciate recontextualized toys. Hopefully, your own child will never seek to represent your parenting in an art museum; it's hardly ever flattering.

CUTE THEN DISTURBING

I always get nervous about cute things in art museums. If you want to see cute things, go to the zoo or the Disney Store. But in an art museum, the cute is almost always step one in a cute-creepy one-two punch. You're lulled into a false sense of security—*Finally, some cute kitty drawings!*—and then you get walloped with the disturbing—*It's eating a baby!* Or again with the penises. Just be careful.

EXIT THROUGH THE GIFT SHOP

Gone are the days when museum gift shops were wastelands of boring books and postcards. Now gift shops are just glorified toy stores. The Met has cute mummy books. MoMA has coloring sets inspired by Rothko. The Guggenheim has special Frank Lloyd Wright Legos. I'd bet you have to go somewhere seriously tragic to avoid toys, like the September 11 Museum or the Holocaust Museum, though I haven't tested that theory yet.

And a lot of these toys your kid is begging for are so gunked up with learning that you know they won't be any fun. Warhol soup-can print-making kits may seem fun, but making pop art is harder than it looks. We've got a REESE'S Peanut Butter Cup problem: We've all become so insistent on toys having educational value that now you can't have educational value without toys! *You got your education in my toy! You got your toy in my education!*

But even if real museums are hard to navigate sometimes, what can you do? Go back to a children's museum?

OTHER KID PERSONALITY TYPES: A GUIDE

At least you're used to your kid's weird personality. But now that you're at the playground, in playgroups, and at preschool, you have to deal with all kinds of pint-size freaks. Other kids are weird! Here's what you're up against.

★ **SPAZZES:** The spaz is one of the most ubiquitous types of kid. Is it even okay to call kids spazzes these days? My autocorrect keeps wanting to correct me: a sure sign that calling someone a "spaz" is out of fashion. But look, without the full psychological break-down of these weirdos, the term "spaz" suffices. Spazzes wheel around, going fucking berserk, spazzing out in ways that drive you nuts.

★ **CREEPS:** Pay attention to your instincts; some kids are creeps. Creeps are always trying to look at your butt and they know about how babies are made before they should. These knuckle draggers aren't to be trusted.

★ **BITERS:** There is a type of feral child that is so pissed at the world that they aren't satisfied with hitting. They are biters. These tiny, toothy animals will try to bite your child and/or you if you get too close. Wild-eyed, squirrelly, and immune to reproach, biters break the skin and run. Beware the biters!

★ **SUPERSMART KIDS:** Do you remember the supersmart kid who won every spelling bee or was always whipping that Rubik's Cube around? Those kids are still with us, and you will encounter them playing *Minecraft* and trading *Magic: The Gathering* cards. Supersmart kids are great when they are on your side, but oh man do they like to rub their smarts in your face. *"I know the name of Columbus's ships!"* Big deal. I know that too: the *Nina*, the *Piñata*, and the *Santa Monica*.

★ **KIDS THAT SEEM OLDER BECAUSE THEY ARE BIG:** Sometimes, you'll meet a kid who's bounding around like a dopey puppy and think, *Spaz.* Then he'll start beating up on a kid, and you'll think, *Bully.* But then he'll start crying about something small, and you'll think, *Huh?* That kid is a kid that seems older because he is big. These behemoths often have the emotional depth of a toddler and the hulking girth of a seventh grader. These non-gentle giants can be dangerous, lacking an awareness of their discombobulating size/ability ratio.

★ **KIDS YOU WISH YOU COULD HANG OUT WITH BECAUSE THEY ARE SUPERCOOL:** Some kids just have personal *flair.* You'll look at some radical little dude sporting his own style at such a young age and think, *Boy, I hope he'll be friends with my kid.* In a non-creepy way, you'll wish you could hang with him yourself. Why doesn't your kid like anime? Who taught this kid to wear a vest and a rope bracelet? Cool hat. This kid is just so *authentic*. Note to self: Buy some Keds.

★ **KILL-KILL-KILL KIDS:** Some kids only want destruction. They see evil opportunities in everything: That magnifying glass is perfect for making fire. Balls are perfect for popping. Slides are for sitting in the middle of and not moving. Kill, kill, kill.

★ **DIRTY KIDS:** All kids are filthy, but some kids are truly gross: snot-smeared faces, dirty clothes, and hands sticky with jelly. Go ahead and feel bad about it, you're not wrong that there's something strange going on, but don't let them touch you. Wave from afar, encourage them to "play in the sprinkler," but don't let them touch your phone.

★ **SWEET, BORING KIDS:** Sometimes you are stuck with kids hanging around who are *perfectly fine*. There's nothing to be irritated about, they are *fine*. It's just . . . they are boring. Don't get me wrong, they're sweet! You want to like them. You do. They're just . . . ugh. These milquetoasts aren't your problem; hopefully they'll find someone boring to bother.

CHAPTER SEVEN

MAN ★ VS. ★ BIG KID

BIG KID, TINY PERSON

WHO IS THIS TINY PERSON?

Remember playing Nintendo for hours without anyone bothering you? Or remember throwing rocks at an old window you found? Or almost breaking your neck riding your dirt bike off a giant rock?

That's the size kid you have now: a big kid. Of course, your child won't be allowed to do such things. The happy insanity of your childhood is much too dangerous.

But your big kid is now in the "known world"—the place where your own memories of childhood become clearer and clearer. The challenges your big kid will deal with are the ones you remember dealing with: what lunch table to sit at, how to fudge your way through homework or get people to like you.

Your big kid has real friends—ones that you didn't pick. And your kid listens to crappy music and has bad taste in TV shows and clothes. And she needs money. And, uh-oh, she's on the Internet.

You knew that your kid would become a real person, her own person, but man is it weird.

One day, when I picked up my daughter from school, she was engrossed in a book. We walked home and she hardly looked up. "How was school?" I asked. "Fine," she answered, but she didn't really hear me. She was too busy reading and walking. This rare event, this reading while walking, is the kind of activity that makes you marvel at the big kid you have. Only a few years ago, this kid couldn't read OR walk. And now she can IGNORE me at the same time. Incredible.

There's something gratifying about just being with your big kid while she ignores you. It must be like a baby bird saying to a mama bird, "I got this," before tumbling out the nest and narrowly avoiding death.

HIDDEN HORROR OF PARENTING: YOUR KID'S BORING STORIES ABOUT STUFF THEY REALLY CARE ABOUT

When I was a kid, I used to come home and read my mom passages from *The Hitchhiker's Guide to the Galaxy*. I'd also inflict upon her the ins and outs of my *Dungeons & Dragons* characters and describe the hilarious antics of *Three's Company*. Yeah, I was a pretty cool kid.

All this to say that children are not good storytellers. They've just mastered the ability to speak, they have opinions, and now this: deep interest in certain things without the storytelling chops to make it interesting.

GIRLS AND BOYS ARE BOTH BORING

Roughly speaking, girls tell boring stories about animals and princesses, and boys tell boring stories about trains and cars. That's a broad generalization, but it's still true. Don't hate the player, hate the boring storyteller.

I've sat through a bunch of descriptions of my daughter's den on *Animal Jam*, an online game where, apparently, you are an animal and can decorate your den. She'll get various special objects to decorate it, and there's some kind of enemy or something. I forget because it's too boring.

I count myself lucky to have a girl. I don't know why I'd rather hear about *Animal Jam* or the ponies of *My Little Pony* than some dumb stuff about Lightning McQueen and his *Cars* friends. Maybe it's because I am a city dweller. I've just never cared about cars or *Cars*.

YOUR KID IS LIKE YOUR MOST ANNOYING COWORKER

Kids will tell you their boring stories because they are enthused and not yet self-aware; it'd be sweet if it weren't so annoying. You don't want to crush a child's interest in something, but if you had a coworker like that, you'd work from home. Kids are supposed to be enthusiastic. It's endearing. Bear that in mind before you yell, "Enough!" and cover your ears.

MAYBE LISTENING TO BORING STORIES = LOVE

Smiling and nodding and saying, "Oh . . . uh-huh," every once in a while to seem like you're listening isn't really that hard. Maybe that's what love is: suffering through these small stories. Think about when you are old and repeating the same boring stories to your half-deaf wife: Won't you want her to be smiling and nodding and saying, "Oh . . . uh-huh"?

Half-listening is a proud tradition of dads everywhere. And when I full-listen, I usually find stuff to give my daughter a hard time about, so it's worth it. Like, in *Animal Jam*, you can be a tiger who owns a cat for a pet. Huh? Doesn't that seem unfair? But I guess some animals are more equal than others.

So be sure to tune in sometimes, at least to gather material for giving your kid the business.

YOU ARE YOUR PARENTS

Oh, man, remember how your dad used to tell you the same thing over and over? Or how your mom used to remind you of stuff you already knew and how you'd yell, "*I ALREADY KNOWWWWWW.*"

They'd nag, and you'd tune them out and do what you wanted anyway. Man, they were annoying! Yeah, that's you now.

You are your parents now. It's jarring when you first realize this. You'll be mid-lecture and you'll become suddenly self-aware, hearing yourself saying the same crap they used to say in just the exact way they used to say it. And you'll desperately want to tell yourself to *please shut up*, but it'll be too late.

YOU NAG LIKE YOUR PARENTS

There's probably nothing worse than continually harping on the same point over and over, but it's biologically programmed into you now. Is it really "nagging" if it's useful information? Yes, yes it is.

YOU REPEAT YOURSELF BECAUSE YOU FORGOT YOU SAID SOMETHING BEFORE

Isn't it horrible to listen to your parents tell you about some former neighbor's mom that you don't remember and how she is moving to Florida? Especially if you've half-listened to the story already.

Anyway, isn't it horrible to listen to your parents tell you about some former neighbor's mom that you don't remember and how she is moving to Florida? Especially if you've half-listened to the story already.

Well, payback is a bitch, because parenting is guaranteed to rot your brain and make you forget that you already told your kid that they are going to after-school on Tuesday because the neighbor they don't know needs you to help to open the door for the movers that are coming at 4:30. *They know.*

YOU SAY "BE CAREFUL" ALL THE TIME

Oh, okay, now I will! Before, I wasn't going to be careful, but now I will! Every time I tell my kid to be careful, it practically dribbles out of my mouth. I can feel how ineffectual, how unnecessary it is. When they're babies, they're always falling down and banging into things. So it's a hard habit to break, for sure, but once they're a big kid, they aren't paying your warnings any mind.

YOU'RE ALWAYS "REMINDING"

Reminding is a sort of low-grade, passive-aggressive bit of nagging wherein you simply "remind" your child to put her homework in her backpack or to brush her teeth. Kids see right through these "helpful hints."

YOU SAY THE SAME DUMB THINGS

And maybe the worst thing is that you find yourself saying the exact same things your parents used to say. It's like some sick "phrase chromosome" has been passed down to you and you are helpless to avoid saying things like:

★ "Get down."
★ "Turn that off."
★ "We have to get outside today."
★ "I have a few errands to run."
★ "It's dinnertime."
★ "What's the magic word?"
★ "That's what's for dinner."
★ "The kitchen's closed."
★ "Easy-peasy, lemon-squeezey."
★ "Home again, home again, jiggity jog."
★ "I said 'no.'"

Maybe your kids will listen to you more than you listened to your own parents. If not, this whole parenting thing is going to be pretty frustrating.

THE INTERNET: HOW YOUR SWEET CHILD WILL LEARN ABOUT TROLLS

We all know the kinds of crazy pervy stuff that you can find on the Internet. I mean, so you've heard.

Point being, you definitely don't want your kid to have full access to the insanity of 4chan or the easy shopping of Amazon. (Unless she's looking to buy another copy of this book for your family and friends. Maybe bookmark it for her.)

I thought I had locked down the Internet sufficiently until the day my daughter, motivated by some girl pride, decided to look up Girls.com.

Luckily, the kind pervs of Girls.com thought to have a splash page with glamorous, heavily made-up ladies of the night instead of a full-on bukkake scene. In any case, I wasn't ready to explain sex, let alone what it is about tentacles that Japanese people find sexy.

So the Internet must be locked up. We all agree? Sure! No sweat. So how do we go about plugging up this leaky boat?

At work they might have done a great job of blocking you from looking at Facebook, forcing you back to your phone, but at home, you don't have that annoying IT guy to help you fix the computers. If anything, *you're* that annoying tech guy.

So how do we keep our children safe?

PARENTAL CONTROLS: REENTERING YOUR PASSWORD OVER AND OVER

Parental controls are the way you manage your child's access to the Internet. How you do so and whether it works at all depends on the device. In our house, we have a couple of laptops, an iPad, and two iPhones. I know, sounds like Apple should send me free stuff for being such a huge fan. They probably have some kind of Apple giveaway for comedy authors who love their stuff, right? I guess what I'm saying is that I'm a huge Apple fan who likes free stuff.

On the laptops, I set up a child user account and parental controls. Couldn't be easier. Of course, the main thing with any parental control is that you will have to override it several times every day. Makes me glad that I set up that twenty-six-character ultrasecure password every expert wanted me to set up.

Here are some reasons I have to override parental controls:

1. To add more time. We thought our daughter only needed an hour of computer time (the daily limit we had set). Turns out, we need her to have "fifteen more minutes" several times each day.

2. To let cookies do their work. Cookies are what tell a site that you've been there before, and it turns out that every dumb site needs me to authorize eight cookies to function properly.

3. Because the parental control thing stops working or something. You know computers: They just bug out on you sometimes. So then you have to troubleshoot. Kind of makes you miss the days when there were no computers. I don't remember my dad running diagnostics on my Lite-Brite.

SAFE-ISH SEARCH

A big problem is that your child will google something innocent and get horrific results. Knowing the Internet, think about what your child will get to see if they google some of the following.

★ Pretty princesses
★ Riding horses
★ Sleeping Beauty
★ Bedtime
★ Fairies
★ Huge trains

Sick, right? That's why you can set up SafeSearch in Google. Theoretically, SafeSearch will only serve up child-friendly results. It does a pretty good job, although it is not fail-safe.

For one thing, Google seems to like to log you out. When Google wants to know who you are, they are very good at that. But when you want to be logged in, they get weirdly bad at it. You have to log in every time (enter twenty-six-character password).

Also, SafeSearch is like your laziest babysitter: When you come home, the dishes won't be done, but your kid will be alive. SafeSearch still serves up some pretty dicey results—scantily clad ladies, suspect "free" game sites, and other dreck—but you probably won't have to explain anything too hardcore.

TEACH YOUR CHILD YOUR PASSCODE

Tablets and phones can be locked up with a passcode so your kid can't just open it up and start playing something. You have to enter the passcode for them.

See the problem? Maybe you're not as easy a mark as I am, but after the sixth time having to unlock an iPad, I'm guessing you're going to teach your kid that passcode. I know, I know: not you. Good for you, pal, for sticking to your guns. But if (when) you fail, eventually, I welcome you to the brotherhood of doing what's expedient.

TRUST: THE ULTIMATE FIREWALL

There's a theory that the best parental control is the trust you build with your child: You trust that they have learned proper judgment from you and will exercise care. Yeah, yeah, that's why you never saw porn until you were a grown-up, right?

ALLOWANCES: HOW KIDS LEARN TO WASTE MONEY

Your kid has to learn about money somehow; that's what allowances are for. Ideally, kids have a little walking-around money to buy a sticker or something and then save the rest. Pretty soon, you have a tiny Warren Buffett on your hands or one of those kid entrepreneurs wowing investors on *Shark Tank*. Sounds good, if it works.

Do allowances teach anything?

SOME EXPERT PROBABLY HAS AN IDEA

Admittedly, I am not a rich man, unless you mean rich in being awesome. Wouldn't it be great if my years as a layabout were mitigated by a fabulously wealthy, money-savvy child? So I've read up on allowances to get advice. One book I read suggested dividing allowances into three jars:

★ **JAR 1:** Spend
★ **JAR 2:** Save
★ **JAR 3:** Donate

I guess the spend jar money is for, DUH, spending. And the save jar is for saving. And the donate jar is for donating. Sorry I explained those jars. It wasn't really necessary.

Anyway, it's a nice idea, encouraging savings, donating, and spending in equal measure. Very noble.

SOME KIDS ARE SQUIRRELS, SOME ARE NOT

Some kids are weird like my wife was as a child: faithfully putting every nickel away in her piggy bank and accumulating quite a haul until her brother "borrowed" it all. Oh well.

But my daughter has never been much of a saver. She'd rather blow her cash on whatever she can as fast as she can. Anything you can buy for $1.37 or so, that's her preference. At that price point, there is nothing but junk. Fifty cents wasted on a crappy keychain from the bubble machine outside the bodega, eighty-seven more cents put toward a bouncy ball that we won't even let her bounce around the apartment, with me footing the extra thirteen cents and tax.

What is this, a math problem? Point is: She's bad with money.

SAVING FOREVER

We try to convince our daughter to save her money. *"You want an American Girl doll? Great, that's sixty dollars. So if you just save your two-dollar allowance for the next, er, thirty weeks you'll . . . um, have enough . . . money."* Okay, that sucks.

Better to live in the moment, right?

But even when she saves up for something, it almost always ends up being a waste: She hardly ever even plays with the toys she does buy. Not when the iPad is around. The American Girl doll becomes just another member of her sad and lonely forgotten toys club.

Or else her money gets converted into some weird online currency like "Gems" in her favorite online game, *Animal Jam*. She'll save eight dollars to buy six thousand gems and a "bonus diamond," whatever that all means.

BIG MONEY BAILOUTS

And sometimes my daughter comes into some "big money." At Christmas, her grandmother sent her forty dollars! That's like six hundred dollars to you and me. She was over the moon, plotting all the stuff she would get.

What does this teach her, except that it is fun to get lucky, better play the lottery, put down big bets, be "in it to win it," move to Vegas, find a sugar daddy, only visit me once a year reluctantly because things at her childhood home seem so "sad and small." No thanks!

It's impossible to ban other people from giving her big payouts, and she can blow it how she wants.

In the end, maybe wasting money is the only way to learn that money isn't nearly as important as being hilarious or getting likes and retweets.

STOP PLAYING WITH YOUR KIDS AND BORE THEM INTO CREATIVITY

There's a lot of pressure on parents to play with their kids. Science tells us that being involved and playing with your kids is one of the most important things you can do for their early development. New Dads *play* with their kids.

It's exhausting.

A certain amount of benign neglect can be good for your kid, right? Especially now that she's a big kid. Is she even still developing? You're out of the woods on that, right? And anyway, sometimes you have to ignore her for your own sanity.

NON-PORTABLE CHILDREN CAN DO THEIR OWN THING

Tiny babies demand to be picked up and held, and you're happy to oblige. Toddlers must be watched constantly so as to avert destruction. Little kids want you to play with them. But now that you have a big kid, this is optional. In rare earlier moments, you've probably seen them playing quietly by themselves or reading books. So the jig is up! They are capable of doing their own things now.

BOREDOM IS A TOOL

When you were a kid, what eventually drove you to create that dangerous homemade slingshot? Boredom, that's what. Boredom is the mother of invention, as they say. Boring your kid into discovering his own creativity is a huge gift. Soon, he will never have a spare moment due to Venmo notifications and social-media "liking" obligations. But for now, he has precious downtime. Wide open, unplanned downtime to figure out something fun to burn.

REDISCOVER "CHILLING"

I've never been into sportsball, so I've missed out on one of the great sanctioned dad-ignores-his-kids activities: watching the game. But in a spare moment, now that I have a big kid, I've turned to ignoring her in pursuit of the old standby: chilling out. I never thought of chilling out as an activity until I had a kid and it disappeared. It is very hard to chill out with a baby or a little kid. But when you have a big kid, chilling out is a cheap and easy activity that doesn't require a babysitter or much planning. I may not be able to go out and do anything, but I can NOT go out and NOT do something. In other words, I can chill.

IF YOU'RE LEANING, YOU'RE CLEANING

You may find that your bored child relentlessly describes their state by repeating "I'm bored, I'm bored," over and over so much that you almost want to play with him to make him shut up. *Do not do this*. Bored kids who "want something to do" should be assigned chores to cure them of this inability to rediscover free play. A threat of scrubbing the bathtub is a sure cure for boredom.

YOUR KID'S WEIRD FRIENDS

Your kid is friends with a bunch of yahoos and psychopaths. Maybe I'm exaggerating a little. But she knows a lot of weird kids, right?

★ **PAUL:** Is it me, or is Paul always trying to show everyone his penis? Anytime I see kids huddled together somewhere, I'm like, "Please don't let it be Paul showing his penis again."

★ **SHARON:** She's always talking in that horrible baby talk. It's all "I'm a wittle baby! Waaaaaaaah." I tried saying, "I can't understand you," but then just decided to never let her come over again. I know she's only eight years old, but c'mon.

★ **SAM:** Seemed like he was being deliberately messy when he ate dinner at our house. Possibly to get attention? I mean, there's no way he could eat like that on a normal night, right? I'd throw up.

★ **CINDY:** Came over for a playdate and immediately wanted snacks. After some popcorn, it was all, "Can we order lunch?" She'd probably rather have a playdate at the cafeteria. It's wrong to hide food from kids, but I'm not letting her eat all of our organic raspberries.

★ **LYLE:** What a huge liar! He came over, knocked over the Lego house your daughter made, and then denied it was him. That's *super weird*, Lyle! We haven't had any other *spontaneous implosions* of Legos around here except when you're over! How very ODD. Perhaps the poltergeist you seem to invoke hates LIARS.

★ **CODY:** I guess it's good to have a creative kid, but why does she always want to "put on a show" for us? Playdates for big kids are so that parents can fuck off and do what they want. Not watch some half-baked fairy tale that you're improvising on the spot. Use a little editorial judgment. I've watched enough of my friends' crappy Internet videos to know when something could be a minute or two shorter.

Okay, okay, is your child perfect? Of course not! But you have to admit:

★ Frankie is so cool and so funny but never wants to eat anything.

★ Russell kept hitting and kicking the ball around, even when you asked him not to.

★ Mona never speaks. You never hear her say anything.

★ Zach won't keep his hands out of his pants.

★ Sarah has strong ideas about our government.

★ Benjamin keeps picking his nose.

★ Billy is a sore loser.

★ Geoff looks just like his dad, like in a freaky way, actually.

★ Diego cries all the time.

★ Alissa shows no emotion ever. Scary.

You know what? I think I hate all kids.

IT HAPPENED TO ME: THE BLACK BOX

Little kids tell you everything, spilling the beans about their weird ideas: "Dada, there are cats who talk and sing." They piece things together in funny ways, but the mysteries are shared with you.

Your big kid though? She can be a black box, a mysterious reservoir of the unknown. You see her thinking about something, but what? Sometimes, it's just kid stuff, but sometimes, it's something deeper. It turns out that she has a rich inner life, but it's hers, not yours.

Little kids and big kids are different. When a little kid cries, it's because she didn't get dessert. When a big kid cries, it might be because she suddenly realized she won't live forever. It also might just be that the book order might not be in until Thursday. When she's staring off into the distance, she could be thinking, *If we all have different opinions, how will we ever achieve real peace and understanding* or *Fart, fart, fart.*

You're used to years and years of figuring out what's wrong, understanding and accessing your kid's inner life. If your kid is upset, you want to know why. It was needing a bottle, then it was a boo-boo, then it was "doesn't want spaghetti again," and now it's . . . mortality? Mean girls at school? Feeling different? Who knows.

And emotions are all out of whack. A few years ago, my stepdad died. He'd been in declining health for a while, but I'd done minimal prepping for my daughter. I didn't know how she would react. So when I told her, she was sad. She gave me a big hug. She lingered, and then she said, "Can I have my electronic time?" This is a girl who sometimes cries at having to wear socks. No crying, no carrying on. It's times like this that kids seem like sociopaths.

But then a few weeks later, her friend accidentally knocked over her sea monkeys. She wailed, she pleaded for them to be saved. It was all out of proportion. The emotions were all right there under the surface somewhere.

And this year, we went to an exhibit where you were supposed to tie a ribbon on a string to send a thought to someone. She wrote something down—a secret thought—to tie to the ribbon. My wife peeked at it, and it said, "I miss you, Papa." Where did that come from? The black box.

You never know what's getting through, what's making a difference. Death, hard family stuff, friendships . . . it's all inner stuff that they might not share with you.

That's the kid growing up, forging her own path, becoming a teenager, locking her door, heading off into the world. That's the kid becoming stoic, becoming shy or secretive. That was the job: set them up for their own lives. But wow, it's hard to see happen. You got her set up, right?

OLD SCHOOL

It's hard to believe that your child has graduated out of preschool. What a wonderful, creative time of growth and discovery. Now that your kid is done with yoga and painting with her toes, it's back to that beloved institution you remember from when you were a kid: *old-school* school.

I remember touring a school near our place on a Friday: *Pizza Day*. The familiar smell of that beloved square-shaped cardboard with tomato sauce that I knew so well from childhood! Like reuniting with an old friend who just got out of the joint, I didn't know if I should be happy or scared. "Just when I thought I was out . . . they pull me back in . . . "

It's all the same as you remember it.

THE OLD PRINCI-PAL

Some of you ne'er-do-wells may remember your principal better than others do. Some of you may find that it's the *exact same principal that punished you.* There's something about being a public-school administrator that freezes your aging in place like some kind of *Game of Thrones* demon king.

But even if the principal is new to you, the kindly visionary who ran your touchy-feely preschool has been replaced by someone who must conform to the Board of Education requirement to be no fun.

THE SAME OLD LUNCH LADIES AND THE CAFETERIA

Lunch ladies are still dishing out tiny weird hamburgers and rocking the hairnets. And the cafeteria is the same, with all the table drama and social dynamics that put you at the table with the new kids and exchange students. Hopefully, your kid will have better luck.

THERE ARE STILL GREAT TEACHERS

All is not lost. There are still some great teachers.

Some teachers, you'll never forget. Mrs. Magoun, my fifth grade teacher, was an absolute inspiration. And I'll never forget old what's-her-face, my fourth grade art teacher.

From that crazy science teacher who wears the bow tie to the beloved kindergarten teacher who lets you hatch chickens in her class, there are still dedicated educators who will make learning fun. Not as fun as preschool, but a little fun.

. . . AND TERRIBLE TEACHERS

But still, there are terrible teachers. You remember them, too, right? Bores who killed your love of learning with their totally inflexible lesson plans? Luckily, you took that as a challenge and pushed even harder, right? I mean, it's unfair to say that your terrible teachers set you on your current life of crime. And your resilient child will be just fine. Probably.

RECESS STILL ROCKS

And don't worry, there's still recess, so your child will get at least twenty minutes of physical activity during school. Kicking balls around, chatting with friends. . . . Kids still play Drop the Handkerchief, Ringolevio, and Hide the Peasant, right?

AUDITORIUMS HAVE NOT BEEN UPGRADED

Assemblies and school plays spent in a cavernous auditorium on wooden seats: That's where I learned to love the theater. Schools still have those same auditoriums, with those same seats and curtains.

Unfortunately, like some postapocalyptic world where civilization has only passed on crumbs of knowledge to the current mutants, no one knows how to get the speakers to work properly or focus a spotlight.

I'M WORRIED: IS SCHOOL OKAY FOR MY PRECIOUS CHILD?

If this sounds too grim or too soon for your kid, rest easy knowing that you will ease your way into school. In Brooklyn, we got the treat of "Half-Day Pre-K," a two-and-a-half hour session of institutional learning, for a full year before any useful schooling. And you'll have the whole summer off! Plenty of time to figure out what to do with your kid again.

HOMEWORK: MAKE "BEING HOME" WORK

If you think back to being a kid, after noogies, homework is probably your number one bummer. And nowadays, homework starts early, sometimes in kindergarten. As far as I remember, my only home-work in kindergarten was being crazy adorable.

The volume of homework builds slowly over the years. Little kids actually like homework at first because it makes them feel like big kids. It's sad to see small children excited about getting homework, knowing what it will eventually become. Don't you get it, kids? Being a big kid is the first step to respectability, putting away the pirate swords and magic wands, and becoming middle management. We can't all be improv teachers like me.

But homework shall not be avoided. It will only get worse.

HOMEWORK IS WORK FOR YOU TO *NOT* DO

Every dad knows that you're not supposed to do your child's homework. But it's not as though your kid can just go off and "do homework." No, your job is to supervise but not help. You know, help but don't *help*. How do you help but not help? I wish I knew. You're supposed to sit nearby and just watch your kid mess up his homework. I guess the theory is that doing homework incorrectly is how kids learn.

Apparently, this is step one of them "making their own mistakes and learning from them." I mean, your kid will eventually have to be responsible for herself, and that includes making mistakes. She'll screw up her math homework, and then she'll start dating the wrong guy, and then she'll move far away and become part of a cult and rob banks, and sometime shortly before you die, she'll come back and apologize and tell you that she "learned from her mistakes." No thanks.

I say you help them. But just a little.

SAVE THE DRAMA FOR YOUR MAMA

In my fantasies, I sit at the kitchen table, catching up on emails or reading the paper, while my child works on some problems nearby. "I've got it!" she declares with a satisfied grin before diving back into a problem. Isn't hard work gratifying?

In my reality, my wife helps with homework. This is because I am not a fan of drama. There is a whole lot of drama around homework, an extra dose of Sturm und Drang that I can't cotton to. So I shirk my duties and let my wife deal. It's not right.

My daughter is a master complainer, a dillydallier of the first order, and a daydreamer. So the drama alternates between grousing, procrastinating, rolling the pencil back and forth until it falls off the table, some far-off gazing, then more grousing. I'm not good at dealing with it.

"Wife?"

TIME IS A CONSTRUCT

My daughter's teachers seem to assign so much homework that there is no way it could actually happen in a day. Every day, it's supposed to be forty-five minutes of reading, ten math sheets, and two pages of reading comprehension, somehow to be finished in the time between after school and dinner. But that's when screen time happens!

THAT'S WHAT AFTER-SCHOOL IS FOR

After-school programs are great for taking the drama of doing homework and placing it in someone else's lap. Let someone else take the heat. Most programs have a little bit of fun and then a little bit of homework time. With everyone stuck doing homework together, your kid might even finish before she comes home. Besides not having any homework, having the homework already done is the easiest way to do homework.

WHAT THE HELL IS MATH NOW?

You remember math . . . vaguely. Sure, basic math is still a part of your life—mostly in the form of subtraction from your wallet—but it probably never occurred to you to know the WHY of math. Well, bad news: Some of your kids will be learning "new math."

MATH IS LIKE READING NOW

Apparently now they talk about "math literacy." Schools want your kid to understand that there is a reason *why* addition works. And that might mean even getting the wrong answer, as long as they understand the process behind it.

Cool! Except I thought math was about getting the right answer. In fact, that's what I liked about math. That's maybe my favorite thing about math. If I wanted "no right answer," I'd do any other thing but math. In writing, in politics, in marriage, there's just NO RIGHT ANSWER.

But math? There's one answer. One. Answer. Not an opinion. Not a perspective. An answer.

Is everything uncertain now? What happened to good old math?

MATH IS STILL MATH, BUT NOW IT'S NEW MATH

Don't get hysterical yet. Sure it can be jarring to look at your kid's homework and not understand how to do a third-grade math problem, but don't worry.

The first Roman dad whose kid came home with modern-day numerals was probably as nervous as you. He was like, "We've been doing math this way for CCCLXIV years! Why change it?"

But now we know how insane that system was, despite how comfortable togas were. So give new math a chance.

NEW MATH IS WHAT YOUR BRAIN DOES IF YOU LET IT

The idea behind new math is to align math with how your brain works instead of memorizing a bunch of arbitrary rules. Let's say you bought a coffee and a delicious scone for $4.60 and gave the hipster barista $20.00. You'd get $15.40 back under both old and new math. But in new math, it's about the *journey, man.*

In old math, you'd stack that shit up:

$20.00
– 4.60
———

First, you'd subtract 0 from 0, and so far so good. Put that 0 down there.

Okay. Then you'd do some funny arbitrary shit. You start crossing out that 2, make it a 1, cross out the first 0, make it a 9, cross out the next 0 and make it a 10. *Like you do.*

Then it's 10 - 6 = 4. Then 9 - 4 = 5. *Holla at ya boy.*

Then, almost done, 1 - 0 = 1. Then put that decimal point down there and you're psyched: $15.40. Perfect!

In new math, you don't stack; you round. You do what your brain would actually do in real life. First, you round that $4.60 up to $5.00 like you're not the cheap bastard you are. Then you take $5.00 out of $20.00. No problem: $15.00. Then you're like, *Oopsie, I actually* am *still a cheap bastard*, and you insist on your $0.40. *Psych!*

So it's not hard; it just looks weird. It's the *why* of math.

NEW MATH AND OLD MATH ARE FRIENDS

The good news is, at least in my child's case, we eventually got back to doing math in a way that I understand. All the other old math stuff is the same: stacking, long division, multiplication. It's great to have an old friend back. So don't worry, old arbitrary, non-sensical math is still a solid friend you can rely on.

HOW TO FIND OUT THAT SCHOOL WAS "FINE" TODAY

"How was school today?" "Fine."

"What happened at school today?" "Nothing."

"You guys do anything fun at school today?" "I don't have to tell you NUTHIN', copper. I ain't saying squat until I see my lawyer."

You're not trying to interrogate your kid, but WTF. *Something* must have happened at school. Unless you have one of those precociously chatty tiny adults, you're going to need tips on finding out what your kid is doing all day now that she won't tell you anything.

SCHOOL *WAS* FINE

That's the first problem: the big, stupid general question you asked. "How was school today?" is broad, generic, and easy to answer: "Fine." Remember school? It WAS fine. Most days weren't bad and they weren't great. They were fine. Not very memorable, not much to speak of. Come to think of it, most of your days are probably fine, too, if you're lucky.

ASK ABOUT STUFF THEY THINK IS IMPORTANT

I like to ask things like "Is Charlotte still sitting at your table?" or "Did the book order come in?" Sure, I'd like to hear her say, "Daddy, I was so inspired by science lab today that I think I'd like to learn more about genetics!" but it's more likely that she's thinking about the kid who threw up during reading.

SOMETIMES YOU ONLY GET ANSWERS
WHEN YOU DON'T ASK QUESTIONS

Asking questions isn't always the best way to get answers. I learn more about my daughter's day on the quiet walks to and from school than any other time. It's like she needs the space to tell me stuff without the pressure of me asking for it. Make sure you provide some time to just listen to your kid.

WANT A BETTER ANSWER? ASK A WEIRDER QUESTION.

Still want to get your kid talking? Try some of these on for size.

★ How was school today, *really*?

★ Tell me one thing you learned today, but use the voice of the teacher you learned it from.

★ Tell me something that made you laugh today. Is it any funnier than this joke: What do you call a fish with no eye? Fsssssh. I'm still the funniest.

★ When were you bored today? I know, *right*?

★ What do you think about . . . HOW WAS SCHOOL TODAY?

★ Where do you play the most at recess? Oh yeah, totally. That's the best place.

★ Who in your class could you have been nicer to? Oh, don't be so hard on yourself.

★ Is there anyone in your class who needs a time-out? How come? Mm-hmm. Wow. That's crazy; I'm calling their parents.

★ Where is the coolest place at the school? Do you think I could still hang there if I dressed up like a kid?

★ If I called your teacher tonight—well I'm not saying I'm going to, this is a hypothetical question. But IF I DID—I'm not going to. You know what, forget it.

★ What do you think you should learn more of at school? Do you think that you're the best judge of that? I mean, you're just a kid.

IS IT OKAY FOR MY KID TO EAT SCHOOL LUNCH?

You've spent years carefully curating your child's food. Or your wife has. Anyway, that time you brought home the cheap hot dogs to make a "Bigfoot's log cabin," you learned your lesson: organic, non-GMO, no-additive, pasture-raised, antibiotic-free, locally cultivated, seasonally appropriate food is the only food for your family.

Pinterest is lousy with bento boxes full of amazing food that I assume a parent definitely made and that the parent's kid definitely appreciated. But you've got shit to do. So now that your kid is in school, is it okay for him to just eat the cafeteria food and let you save a bunch of time and money and let all the suffering of preparing lunches stop? Sure it is.

THE PROUD TRADITION OF EATING CRAP

We might not have many traditions left in this country, but school lunch is one that we can pass down to our children just the way we remember it.

There it is: all the same crap you ate. Salisbury steak—the duke of Salisbury's gravy-choked meat mound. Tiny, gray steamed hamburgers plucked from a heated tray and deposited on a soggy bun. And I'll say it again: that delicious, wonderful square pizza.

And that's not all:
★ Probably totally fine fish sticks
★ Tater Tots™
★ "Mozzarella" sticks
★ Fruit in a cup with sugar sauce
★ Pudding cups
★ Milk, blessed milk
★ Those soft little rolls

It's all there. I'm getting hungry just listing it.

BUT THERE ARE NEW WEIRD THINGS

You never had seaweed or kale chips for a snack when you were a kid. Food has changed! And the cafeteria food has changed, too. Now there are more options and healthier choices for your precious child. Here are just some of the new food options for your kid to ignore.

- ★ **SALAD BAR:** He can ignore the lettuce and stock up on the weird bacon bits. Or he can put together a nice salad and then smother it with dressing like you do at that midtown hot bar you go to.
- ★ **ZUCCHINI STICKS:** They are like french fries, but instead of using "potatoes," they use "zucchini." I guess that's better?
- ★ **BREADED CHICKEN BITES:** Hmmm, these sound a lot like—you know what, never mind.

LET "DOESN'T LIKE IT" BE SOMEONE ELSE'S PROBLEM

Who knows what your kid likes to eat these days anyway? He doesn't. All you probably know is what he "doesn't like." Great! You don't like turkey anymore? What about ham? No? Or how about carrots? Those don't work either, huh. Well, fuck it! Let the lunch ladies deal with your tiny foodie and his rarified tastes. There are no guarantees that he'll like what's on order that day, but at least it won't be your problem.

LET KIDS MAKE THEIR OWN MISTAKES, STARTING AT LUNCH

Your kid isn't a little kid anymore. He needs to start to own his choices and make his own mistakes. I have the opposite of a fond memory of eating a huge bag of candy corn when I was a child and yacking it all over the place. It was horrible. I learned my lesson: Only eat half of a huge bag of candy corn at a time.

RANCH DRESSING IS A GATEWAY DRUG

There's a danger in being too virtuous and teaching your kids that vegetables suck. When I was a kid, a vegetable wasn't a vegetable without a cream or cheese sauce. The seventies and eighties were a golden era of thick, gooey sauces that tasted great. So you don't want that for your child? Me neither. But sometimes the ranch dressing makes the carrot go down, and cafeterias always have sauces. Sure, you come for the ranch, but eventually maybe you develop a taste for the carrot.

MONEY AND FOOD DOESN'T GROW ON TREES

Wasting time, money, and food: That has to be the worst threesome imaginable. How annoying is it to have a carefully packed lunch sent off in the morning only to have it return in the afternoon untouched or barely pecked at? Save your money, save your time, and save your loving relationship with the little shitheel who won't eat your lovely lunches. Let them eat school lunch!

IT HAPPENED TO ME: FISH STICKS

ME: "Do they ever serve fish at school?"

DAUGHTER: "Not fish, but they do have FISH STICKS!"

ME: "Oh, cool."

DAUGHTER: "Um . . . Except they don't have FISH in them. They have CHEESE."

ME: "Those are cheese sticks."

DAUGHTER: "Yep, that's what we have: cheese sticks."

UPCOMING SCHOOL CALENDAR

Parents should be aware of some upcoming dates when school will not be in session!

WEEK OF NOVEMBER 12–16

★ **MONDAY:** No School – Veterans Day

★ **WEDNESDAY:** Half Day – Teachers' Conference

★ **THURSDAY:** Half Day – Book Fair (Or something else sketchily described a long time ago that you forgot to read about. Put $5 in your kid's folder, you ingrate!)

WEEK OF NOVEMBER 19–23

★ **WEDNESDAY:** Early Dismissal – No Reason (Don't forget unless you are a bad parent.)

★ **THURSDAY:** No School – Thanksgiving

★ **FRIDAY:** No School – Thanksgiving

WEEK OF NOVEMBER 26–30

★ **MONDAY:** Quarter day – Leftovers Day

★ **WEDNESDAY:** No School – "Why Have School?" Day

★ **THURSDAY:** No School – Snow Day (or a Hurricane/ Storm/There's No Gas or Something Day)

WEEK OF DECEMBER 3–7

- ★ **TUESDAY:** No School – Christmas Shopping Day
- ★ **WEDNESDAY:** Early Dismissal – Just to Fuck with You
- ★ **THURSDAY:** Full Day (But now you're spooked right? Pick up early to be safe.)

WEEK OF DECEMBER 10–14

- ★ **MONDAY:** No School – Hanukkah?
- ★ **TUESDAY:** No School – Hanukah (I spelled it different this time, so no school this day either.)
- ★ **WEDNESDAY:** No School – Yom Kippur (Though I'm pretty sure that already happened.)
- ★ **FRIDAY:** No School – Gray Friday

WEEK OF DECEMBER 17–21

- ★ **ALL WEEK:** No School – Just 'Cause

WEEKS OF DECEMBER 24–MARCH 26

- ★ **NO SCHOOL:** Christmas/New Year's Day/Presidents' Day/MLK Day/Mid-Winter Break

TIME TO VOLUNTEER, DAD

Now that dads are New Dads, you are expected to do some seriously boring bullshit.

There was a time when moms had to do all the heavy lifting: Parent-Teacher Organization (PTO), bake sales, volunteering at school. Oh yeah, it's still that time. But now the PTO wants you, too.

Maybe you're already involved in other ways. Perhaps you are a coach of your kid's team or you are a scoutmaster or something. Yeah, yeah, yeah. That's great, but that's all dad stuff that we knew you'd do. Now you have to do all that PTO/mom shit like fundraising and chaperoning.

FUNDRAISING: STONES AND THE MONEY SQUEEZED FROM THEM

Schools never get enough money for things. Are you good with money? Do you have money? Neither? Oh well. Schools can't seem to get money from the government, so it has come down to you.

But they aren't going to just come out and ask for money over and over. They will disguise these requests in the form of events and fundraisers:

★ **BAKE SALES:** You or your wife will spend precious time and money on delicious organic ingredients for your special vegan raspberry bars. These will be passed over in favor of marshmallow treats.

★ **CANDY SALES AND OTHER BS:** My daughter had to deal with this old-school racket in which your child sells overpriced candy to your relatives with the promise that if she sells twenty billion candy bars, she'll get an iPad. Needless to say, this never happens. Pretty sweet for the company to get a free sales force for their junk, though!

★ **THE SPRING GALA AUCTION:** This is where everyone pretends they have money, gets you drunk, and makes you bid on shit you don't want. Seems like a sober person wouldn't have spent eighty bucks on a muffin breakfast with the principal, but then again, you were not a sober person.

YOUR SKILL SET, TIME, AND PRESENCE IS REQUESTED

Can you build things? Or cook? Or, God forbid, do you own a T-shirt shop or something? These and other skills will be helpful to the PTO. Bet you're wishing you were a comedian like me now.

And the PTO would also like you to attend the events. There are talent shows, school plays, bake sales, hoe downs, auctions, and fairs.

Perhaps you would chaperone? You could relive the horrors of school dances, but ya know, for a good cause this time.

EPILOGUE

Guys, I hope this has been helpful—or at least funny. I really hope I was right in not making this whole thing look like a drill manual or something.

I've been a dad for ten years now. If I have my math correctly, that means I'm ten years older than I was when my daughter was born. It feels like a long time ago. But *oh the memories* . . .

I remember toting her around in her BabyBjörn, feeling like a busty lady because people were always staring at my chest. *My eyes are up here, buddy.*

And then I remember coloring with her at her tiny watercolor-stained table—and not in any of those fancy "adult coloring books" like they have now, in big, stupid *Dora the Explorer* coloring books. And I'd get yelled at if I made Boots's boots anything but red.

And, of course, I remember awkwardly texting her friend's mom to see if she could FaceTime with her friend like I was some kind Internet chaperone. I remember that because it happened last week.

So I'm older, but am I wiser? I think I am. Being a dad has been the most incredible thing that could happen to me, except maybe getting superpowers from an industrial chemical accident, but who knows if that will ever happen. I can only break into that factory so many times.

Here are some things I have learned from having a kid.
- ★ Being ready for a kid is overrated.
- ★ I'm a better person when I open myself up.
- ★ There's a lot of beauty out there if you look at things like kids do.
- ★ Being fun is more fun than not being fun, duh.

But that's about all the time I have for introspection. It's all been such a rush for so long. Where has the time gone? How did I get so old? Is that brunch place still open?

For the last few years, I've been steadily getting my freedom back. Sometimes, I can play a game on my phone without knowing where my kid is at that very moment, unafraid that she will fall and kill herself and my wife will blame me. But isn't freedom its own kind of prison? Being needed can be nice.

It's true that my kid is still a kid, but barely. She's almost a tween and then a teen, and then she'll move away and forget me. The signs are all there: she knows my log-ins, she arranges her own playdates, I embarrass her. The handwriting is on the wall, and I leave it there because it reminds me of her when she was little. Look, she misspelled *fart*. Sigh.

A teenager! Scary thought, right? Teenagers are the same monsters that take over a full subway car and show off by doing eight hundred pull-ups. They're exuberant and smell funny. I'll take a little kid any day.

When my daughter was little, we would walk to the playground a few blocks away. This would take forty-five minutes because there was so much to see on the journey. At one house, there was a ceramic frog in the front garden. We had to say hi to him: "Hi, Mr. Frog!" There were gum wrappers to try to pick up. There were stones to jump and balance on.

But teenagers are in a hurry. Mr. Frog's like, "Hey, remember me?" My daughter: "Ew, whatever." They're on their way to being grown-ups. And you just want them to slow down, stay with you a little longer.

I know my daughter is actually the same wackadoo kid underneath. She's still sweet and funny, but now she'll surprise me by being sarcastic too. *My girl.* And she still wants a hug after a bad day.

I guess even teenagers need a dad, maybe they even *especially* need a dad. Maybe the best years are to come: years when I can really hone my uncoolness into being an enthusiastically embarrassing dad.

I sure hope so.

ACKNOWLEDGMENTS

I would like to thank, first and foremost, my wonderful family. My daughter is a kind, funny kid who has expanded my heart. Without her it would have been super weird to write a book about being a dad. And without my wife, I would have been too insane to write a book at all. I didn't give her enough credit, but *Man and More Competent Wife vs. Child* was a terrible title. I love you both. It's been an extraordinary time and I've been so lucky to be able to share it with you.

Thanks also to my gentle editor Rebecca Kaplan for patiently listening to me argue for things that I eventually cut anyway, once I realized she was right. Thanks to my agent Jud Laghi for his faith in me and his expert guidance in realizing this book. Needless to say, without the incredible design and production team at Abrams this would be an unreadable mess. Thanks for making it inviting.

Jordan Awan's illustrations are so great, aren't they? You should have seen the crappy doodles that I dumped in his lap. He made some of that junk into real gems and brought so many of his own warm and witty ideas to my book.

Thanks to the UCB community for letting me abuse their years of friendship with outsized requests for help. Special thanks to Cody Lindquist, Rachael Mason, Kerry McGuire, Dan Hodapp, Lydia Hensler, Ann Carr, Molly Lloyd, Betsy Capes, Geoff Garlock, Sarah Rainone, Dawn Luebbe, Steve Collins, Scott Moe, Marc Liepis, and Sherief Elkatsha.

Thank you to my parents who made me who I am and who helped me pass down good things to my daughter.

Finally, thanks to all the parents out there, especially the funny ones. You still got it!

Editor: Rebecca Kaplan
Designer: Danielle Young
Production Manager: Alex Johnson

Library of Congress Control Number: 2016946248

ISBN: 978-1-4197-2399-5

Printed and bound in the United States
10 9 8 7 6 5 4 3 2 1

Abrams books are available at special discounts when purchased in quantity
for premiums and promotions as well as fundraising or educational use.
Special editions can also be created to specification. For details, contact
specialsales@abramsbooks.com or the address below.

ABRAMS The Art of Books
115 West 18th Street, New York, NY 10011
abramsbooks.com